THEATER CRITICS RAVE ABOUT

ALL OVER:

"**The best American play of several seasons.**"
—Harold Clurman, *The Nation*

"Without question the best-written, the most mature, the most deeply felt and the most sensitively wrought drama Albee has written so far. And without question, it's the best play—American and British—of this and many past seasons. It restores faith in the American Theater —and re-establishes Broadway as an artistic forum and Edward Albee as our foremost dramatist." —Samuel Hirsch, *Boston Herald Traveler*

"**A boldly beautiful and quietly brilliant play.**"
—Elliot Norton, *Boston Record American*

"*All Over* stands as the most original and finest *coup de théâtre* of American origin this season."
—William Glover, Associated Press

ALL OVER
was originally published by Atheneum.

EDWARD ALBEE

ALL OVER

A PLAY

PUBLISHED BY POCKET BOOKS NEW YORK

ALL OVER

Atheneum edition published 1971

POCKET BOOK edition published March, 1974

L

This POCKET BOOK edition includes every word contained in the original, higher-priced edition. It is printed from brand-new plates made from completely reset, clear, easy-to-read type. POCKET BOOK editions are published by POCKET BOOKS, a division of Simon & Schuster, Inc., 630 Fifth Avenue, New York, N.Y. 10020. Trademarks registered in the United States and other countries.

Standard Book Number: 671-78406-4.
Library of Congress Catalog Card Number: 71-162965.
This POCKET BOOK edition is published by arrangement with Atheneum Publishers. Copyright, ©, 1971, by Edward Albee. All rights reserved. This book, or portions thereof, may not be reproduced by any means without permission of the original publisher: Atheneum Publishers, 122 East 42 Street, New York, N.Y. 10017.

Printed in the U.S.A.

FOR

Bernard and Rebecca Reis

FIRST PERFORMANCE
March 27, 1971, Martin Beck Theater, New York City

JESSICA TANDY *as* THE WIFE
MADELEINE SHERWOOD *as* THE DAUGHTER
COLLEEN DEWHURST *as* THE MISTRESS
NEIL FITZGERALD *as* THE DOCTOR
JAMES RAY *as* THE SON
GEORGE VOSKOVEC *as* THE BEST FRIEND
BETTY FIELD *as* THE NURSE
JOHN GERSTAD, CHARLES KINDL, *and* ALLEN WILLIAMS
as TWO PHOTOGRAPHERS AND A REPORTER

THE CHARACTERS

THE WIFE *71; small-boned, not heavy.
Dresses well, if conservatively; gray-
haired, probably.*

THE MISTRESS *61; auburn or dark
blond hair; a great beauty fading
some; more voluptuous than* THE
WIFE, *maybe a bit taller; given to
soft, pastel clothes.*

THE SON *52; a heavy-set man, soft
features; dark hair, business clothes.*

THE DAUGHTER *45; angular; once at-
tractive, now a little ravaged; doesn't
care much about how she dresses.*

THE BEST FRIEND *73; an erect, good-
looking gray-haired man, thin to
middling; well dressed, well
groomed.*

THE DOCTOR *86; a tiny, shrunken
white-haired man; needn't be tiny,
but it would be nice.*

THE NURSE *65; a large woman, gray-
streaked blond hair; wears a nurse's
uniform.*

TWO PHOTOGRAPHERS AND A REPORTER;
*no matter, middle-aged, or whoever
understudies the male principals.*

ONE IDEA OF A SET: *A paneled bed-sitting room. The bed—a huge, canopied four-poster on a raised platform to the rear. Back there, an armoire, perhaps a bureau, a hospital stand for instruments and medicines, a hospital screen hiding the occupant of the bed. In the sitting-room part, a huge fireplace in the stage-right wall, and a door leading to a bath-room upstage of it. In the stage-left wall, a door leading to the hall. The room is solid and elegant, a man's room. The furniture, all of which is good and comfortable, is most probably English. Several chairs, a sofa, side tables, lamps. A tapestry, eighteenth-century family portraits. An Oriental carpet.*

TIME: *The present.*

ACT ONE

THE DOCTOR *at the bed with the patient;* THE
NURSE *at the foot of the bed. The others
about, the three women probably sitting,* THE
SON *and* THE BEST FRIEND *maybe not.
Unless otherwise indicated, the characters
will speak in a conversational tone, without
urgency, more languorously than not. But
there will be no whispering; the languor is
not boredom, but waiting. The fireplace has
an ebbing fire in it; the room is warm.*

THE WIFE
(*Gazing at the fire*)

Is he dead?

THE DAUGHTER
(*A gentle admonishment: not a rebuke*)

Oh, mother.

15

THE DOCTOR

Hunch.

THE BEST FRIEND
(*More curiosity than reproach*)
Don't you *want* to be here?

THE DAUGHTER
(*Considering it for the first time*)
Well . . . I don't *know*.
(THE MISTRESS *laughs gently*)

THE BEST FRIEND
It's not required that you *do* know. It *is* more or less
required that you *be* . . . I think: here. Family. Isn't
it one of our customs? That if a man has not outlived
his wife and children—will not outlive them . . . they
gather?

THE WIFE
(*To* THE BEST FRIEND)
And his closest friend, as well.
(THE BEST FRIEND *bows slightly, cocks his
head*. THE WIFE *indicates* THE MISTRESS)
And don't forget *her*.

THE BEST FRIEND
(*Matter-of-fact, but friendly*)
And his . . . very special friend, too.

THE MISTRESS
(*Smiles*)
Thank you.

18

THE BEST FRIEND

And we do it—custom—wanted, or not. We wait until
we cannot be asked—unless there is something written,
or said, refusing it—and we . . . gather, often even *if*
we are refused.

THE WIFE

And is that *so?* In your lawyerish way . . .

THE BEST FRIEND

No; we have not been refused.

THE WIFE
(*To* THE DOCTOR)

A hunch. *Nothing* more . . . technical than that? More
medical? Your hunch it will be *soon?* Your intuition
if you were a woman, or are doctors graced with that?
(*To her* DAUGHTER; *somewhat chiding*)
We've not *come* any distance. Is it just we're in the
room with him—not at the hotel, or downstairs?

THE DAUGHTER

I suppose. And that we lived here once.

THE WIFE
(*To* THE DAUGHTER)

That was another century.
(*To* THE DOCTOR)

Hunch.

THE DOCTOR
(*To* THE WIFE)

I can't give it to you to the minute. Did I predict when
she would be born?

                    (*Refers to* THE DAUGHTER)
The hour—the day, for that matter? Or him?
                    (*Refers to* THE SON)

                    THE MISTRESS
                    (*Back to the point*)
Though you have *reason*.

                    THE DOCTOR
Yes.
                         (*Pause*)

                    THE WIFE
        (*A little as though she were speaking to a
        backward child*)
And what *is* it?

                    THE NURSE
            (*Fact more than reproach*)
You should let him die in the hospital.

                    THE DAUGHTER
Yes!

                    THE WIFE
                (*Quietly indignant*)
Hooked up?

                    THE NURSE
                    (*Shrugs*)
Whatever.

THE MISTRESS

(Soft-smiling; shaking her head; faintly ironic)
Yes, of course we should have.
(*To* THE WIFE)
Can you imagine it?

THE WIFE

Tubes; wires. All those machines, leading to and from?
A central gadget?
(*To them all, generally*)
That's what he had become, with all those tubes and
wires: one more machine.
(*To* THE MISTRESS)
Back me up.

THE MISTRESS

Oh, far more than *that*.

THE WIFE

A city seen from the air? The rail lines and the roads?
Or, an octopus: the body of the beast, the tentacles
electrical controls, recorders, modulators, breath and
heart and brain waves, and the tubes!, in either arm
and in the nostrils. Where had he gone!? In all that . . .
equipment. I thought for a moment *he* was keeping
it . . . functioning. Tubes and wires.

THE NURSE

They help to keep time, to answer your questions
easier.
(*Shakes her head*)
That's all.

21

THE MISTRESS

The questions are very simple now. A stopwatch should do it, a finger on the wrist . . .

THE DAUGHTER
(*Fairly arch*)

We are led to understand . . .

THE MISTRESS
(*No nonsense*)

He *said* . . . *here*.

THE DAUGHTER
(*None too pleasant*)

We have your word for it.

THE WIFE
(*Shrugs*)

We have her word for *everything*.

THE MISTRESS
(*Not rising to it*)

He *said* . . . *here*. When it becomes hopeless . . . no, is that what he said? Pointless! When it becomes point-less, he said . . . have me brought back here. I want a wood fire, and a ceiling I have memorized, the knowledge of what I could walk about in, *were* I to. I want to leave from some place . . . I have known.
(*Changed tone; to* THE DAUGHTER)
You have my *word* for it; yes, you have only my word . . . for so very much . . . if he loved you, for ex-ample . . . **any** more.
(*To them all; triste*)
You *all* have my word, and that is all. I translate for

22

you, as best I can; I tell you what I remember, or
think I remember, and I lie sometimes, and give you
what he would have said . . . *had* he: thought to . . .
or bothered.

THE DAUGHTER
(*Dogged, but not forceful*)

That will not do.

THE SON
(*Quiet*)

Please?

THE DAUGHTER
(*Scoffing*)

You!

THE WIFE

When I came there, to the hospital—the last time,
before the . . . removal here—I said . . .
(*Turns to* THE MISTRESS)
you were not there, were shopping, or resting, I
think . . .
(*Turns back generally*)
looking at him, all wired up, I stood at the foot of the
bed—small talk all gone, years ago—I shook my head,
and I clucked, I'm afraid—tsk-tsk-tsk-tsk—for he
opened his eyes a little, baleful, as I suppose my gaze
must have seemed to him, though it was merely . . .
objective. This won't do at all, I said. Wouldn't you
rather be somewhere else? Do you want to be here?
He kept his eyes half open for a moment or so, then
closed them, and nodded his head, very slowly. Well,
which?, I said, for I realized I'd asked two questions,

23

and a nod could mean either yes or no. Which is it?, I said; do you want to be here? Slow shake of the head. You *would* rather be somewhere else. Eyes opened and closed, twice, in what I know—from eons—to be impatience; then . . . nodding. Well, naturally, I said, in my bright business tone, of course you don't want to be here. Do you want to go home? No reply at all, the eyes burning at me. Your own home, I mean, not mine certainly. Or hers. Perhaps you want to go there. Shall I arrange something? Eyes still on me, no movement. Do you want *her* to arrange it? Still the eyes, still no movement. Has it been arranged? Has she arranged it already? The eyes lightened; I could swear there was a smile in them. She *has*. Well; good. If it is done, splendid. All I care is whether it is *done*. I no longer feel possessive, have not for . . . and the eyes went out—stayed open, went out, as they had . . . oh . . . so often; so far back.

(To THE MISTRESS)

That is one of those things . . .

THE DAUGHTER
(Possessive, in a very female way)

MOTHER!

THE WIFE

Do not . . . *deflect* me.

THE DAUGHTER
(More a whine, but protective)

MOTHER.

THE WIFE
(As cool as possible)

Yes?

24

(*Pause*)
Out. Stayed open, went out.

THE MISTRESS
Ah, well; that happened often.

THE WIFE
(*Quiet, almost innocent interest*)
Yes?

THE MISTRESS
Ah; well, yes.

THE WIFE
Odd I don't remember it. The opening and closing . . .
of course, the . . . impatience, but . . . out.

THE MISTRESS
(*Gently*)
Ah, well; perhaps you should have noticed. It must
have happened.

THE WIFE
(*A small smile*)
Well, yes, perhaps I should have. Doubtless it did.

THE MISTRESS
It was always—for me . . .

THE DAUGHTER
Was? The past tense? Why not *is*?

THE MISTRESS
(*Not rising to it; calm*)

He has not, for some time. You *were* a little girl. Are you still?

> (THE DAUGHTER *turns away*)

THE WIFE
> (*A little laugh*)

Semantics from a C minus?

THE SON
> (*Softly*)

Leave her alone.

THE WIFE
> (*Not harsh*)

Was it not? At school? A C minus, if that? *You* were little better.

THE MISTRESS

It was always—for me—an indication that . . .

THE DOCTOR
> (*No urgency*)

Nurse.
> (*Some reaction from them all; not panic, but a turning of heads; a quickening*)

THE WIFE
> (*A little breathless*)

Something?

THE DOCTOR
> (*Looks up at them; a slight smile; some surprise*)

Oh . . . oh, *no*. Just . . . business.
> (*Slight pause*)

THE MISTRESS
(*Not pressing; continuing*)
. . . an indication that . . . some small fraction had gone
out of him, some . . . faint shift from total engagement.
Or, if not that, a warning of it: impending.

THE WIFE
(*A smile*)
Ah. Then I *do* know it . . . the sense of it, and probably
from what you describe, without knowing I was aware
of it.

THE BEST FRIEND
I have been aware of it.

THE WIFE
(*Referring to her husband*)
In *him?*

THE BEST FRIEND
No. In myself.

THE WIFE
(*Mildly mocking*)
You *have?*

THE BEST FRIEND
(*Smiles*)
Yes; I have.

THE WIFE
(*Smiling, herself*)
How extraordinary.
(*Thinks about it*)
When?

27

THE BEST FRIEND
(*To* THE WIFE)

In relation to my wife, when I was wavering on the divorce, during that time you and I were—how do they put it?—comforting one another; that secret time I fear that everyone knew of.

THE MISTRESS

He never knew of it. *I* did. I didn't tell him.

THE WIFE
(*Sad; smiling*)

Well, there wasn't very much to tell.

THE BEST FRIEND

No; but some; briefly. It was after I decided not to get the divorce, that year . . . until I committed her. Each thing, each . . . incident—uprooting all the roses, her hands so torn, so . . . killing the doves and finches . . . setting fire to her hair . . . all . . . all those times, those things I knew were pathetic and not wanton, I watched myself withdraw, step back and close down some portion of . . .

THE MISTRESS

Ah, but that's not the same.

THE WIFE
(*Not unkindly; objectively*)

No, not at all; she was *insane* . . . your wife.

THE MISTRESS

And that is not what we meant at all.

THE WIFE

No, not at all.

THE BEST FRIEND

It is what you were talking about.

THE MISTRESS
(*Laughs a little; sadly*)

No. It's when it happens calmly and in full command: the tiniest betrayal—nothing so calamitous as a lie held on to in the face of fact, or so niggling as a fantasy during the act of love, but in between—and it can be anything, or nearly nothing, except that it moves you back into yourself a little, the knowledge that all your sharing has been . . .

THE WIFE

. . . arbitrary . . .

THE MISTRESS

. . . willful, and that nothing has been inevitable . . . or even necessary. When the eyes close down; go out.

THE SON
(*Intense*)

My father is dying!

THE WIFE
(*After a tiny pause*)

Yes. He is.

THE DOCTOR

If you want to go back downstairs, any of you . . .

THE DAUGHTER

. . . to the photographers? The people from the papers?
I put my foot on the staircase and they're all around
me: Has it happened yet? *Is* he? May we go up now?
Eager. Soft voices but very eager.

THE WIFE
(*Soothing*)

Well, they have their families . . . their wives, their
mistresses.

THE DAUGHTER
(*Generally*)

Thank you: I'll stay up here; I'll sit it out.

THE WIFE
(*With a wrinkling of her nose*)

Neat.

THE DAUGHTER
(*Slightly incredulous*)

Did you say neat?

THE MISTRESS

Yes; she did.

THE DAUGHTER
(*To her mother*)

Because I said sit it out?

THE WIFE
(*Without expression; waiting*)

Um-humm.

THE DAUGHTER
(Startlingly shrill)
WELL, WHAT ARE YOU DOING!?

THE WIFE
(Looks up at her, smiles vaguely, speaks softly)
I am waiting out a marriage of fifty years. I am waiting
for my *hus*band to *die*. I am thinking of the little girl I
was when he came to me. I am thinking of . . . do you
want me to stop? . . . almost everything I can except
the two of you—you and your . . . unprepossessing
brother—
(Light, to THE SON*)*
Do forgive me.
(Back)
I am sitting it out. *I* . . . am sitting it out.
(To THE DAUGHTER*)*
And *you* are?

THE DAUGHTER
Enjoying it less than you.

THE MISTRESS
(To THE DAUGHTER; *a quiet discovery; as if
for the first time, almost)*
You are not a very kind woman.

THE WIFE
(Passing it off)
She has been raised at her mother's knee.

THE DAUGHTER
(To THE MISTRESS*)*
And am I suddenly *your* daughter?

31

THE MISTRESS

Oh; my stars! No!

THE DAUGHTER

Well, you have assumed so much . . .

THE WIFE
(*Announcement of a subject*)

The little girl I was when he came to me.

THE MISTRESS

So much?

(*To* THE WIFE)

Interesting: it's only the mother who can ever really know whose child it is. Well, the husband knows his wife is *having* the baby . . .

THE WIFE
(*Laughs gaily*)

He took me aside one day—before you and he had made your liaison; they were grown, though—and, rather in the guilty way of "Did I *really* back the car through the *whole* tulip bed?", asked me, his eyes self-consciously focusing just off somewhere . . . "*Did* I make these children? Was it *our* doing: the two of us alone?" I laughed, with some joy, for while we *were* winding down we were doing it with talk and presence: the silences and the goings off were later; the titans were still engaged; and I said, "Oh, yes, my darling; yes, we did; they are our very own."

(*She chuckles quietly.*

Brief pause; THE DAUGHTER *rises, almost languidly, walks over to where* THE WIFE *is sitting, slaps her across the face, evenly, without*

32

*evident emotion, returns to where she is sit-
ting.*

After a pause; to THE MISTRESS*; small smile*)
Excuse me.

(*She rises, just as languidly, walks over to
where* THE DAUGHTER *is sitting, slaps her
across the face, evenly, without evident emotion, returns to where she is sitting. After a
noncommittal sigh at* THE DAUGHTER, *who is
glaring straight ahead, over her shoulder, to*
THE DOCTOR)

And what do you think now?

THE DOCTOR
(*Patient smile*)

Are you back at my intuition again? My hunch? Your
funny names for all the years I've watched you come
and go? Both your parents, both of his. My sixty years
of practice.

(*Indicates* THE NURSE)

The forty years she's come here with me to sit up nights
with you all?

THE WIFE

Yes.

THE MISTRESS
(*Some wonder*)

Sixty years of *something*.

THE WIFE
(*Still to* THE DOCTOR)

Even on the chance of frightening the horses, or being

33

taken as heartless—which I am *not*—are you holding
him back, or are you seeing him through to it?
  (THE DAUGHTER *stiffens, turns on her heel,
  moves to the door, opens it, exits, slams it
  after her*)

THE DOCTOR
  (*Watching this before he answers*)
I've stopped the intravenous feeding. We're letting him
. . . starve, if you will. He's breathing very slowly now
. . . like sleep. His heart is . . .
  (*Shrugs*)
. . . well, weak . . . bored is close to it. He's bleeding
. . . internally. Shall I go on?

THE WIFE
  (*No expression*)
Please do.

THE DOCTOR
If you'd like to come and look . . . he seems to have
diminished every time I turn my head away and come
back. There'll be precious little left for the worms.

THE MISTRESS
The flames.

THE WIFE
  (*Having heard something on the wind*)
Oh? Yes?

THE MISTRESS
He will be burned. "And you are not to snatch my heart
from the flames," he said, "for it is not a tasty organ."

34

THE WIFE
(*Schoolmarmish*)
Per*haps*. Per*haps* he will be burned.

THE BEST FRIEND
(*Quite serious; really!*)
Surely he didn't suggest an outdoor event . . . a funeral
pyre!
(*He is stopped by a concert of* THE WIFE *and*
THE MISTRESS *in rather cold, knowing, help-
less laughter*)

THE SON
(*Finally*)
Don't you . . . *have* something? Some papers?

THE WIFE
(*Rather helpless in quiet, terrible laughter*)
You *must!*

THE SON
(*Doubtless the most intense in his life*)
You MUST!

THE MISTRESS
Yes!

THE BEST FRIEND
(*After an embarrassed pause*)
There . . . *are* . . . papers . . . envelopes I've not
opened, on instruction; there may be . . .

THE MISTRESS
(*Adamant; cool*)
It was a verbal . . . envelope.

35

THE BEST FRIEND
I will go by what is *down*.

THE WIFE
(Half sardonic, half leaning)
Of *course* he will.

THE MISTRESS
(Cold; a diamond hardness, yet womanly)
Oh, Christ; you people! You will go by what I tell you;
finally; as I have told you.

THE WIFE
(Almost as if improvising; bright)
No! We will go with what *is*, with what resides. Good-
ness, if a man desires to go up in flames, let him put it
down—on a tablet! Or shall we go over and shake him
. . . wake him to the final glory before the final glory,
and have two women at him, with a best friend over-
head, and make him make his *mind* up! "My darling,
we merely want to know! Is it flame or worm? Your
mistress tells me you prefer the flame, while I, your
merely wife of fifty years, the mother of your doubted
children—true, oh, true, my darling—wants you to the
worms. Do tell us. Yes? Open your awful lips for a
moment, or do your eyes: open and close them, put
them on and out; let us . . . finally! . . . misunderstand."
(THE MISTRESS *smiles, slowly applauds. Five
sounds; seven; always an odd number.*
*Brief pause following the applause, during
which* THE WIFE *nods her head gently toward*
THE MISTRESS)

36

THE DOCTOR
(*To himself, but not sotto voce*)
Death is such an old disease.
(*Realizes he is being listened to; speaks to*
THE WIFE *and* THE MISTRESS, *laughs a little*)
That being so, it must be a comfort having someone as
old as I am by the bed: familiar with it, knowing it so
well.

THE MISTRESS
Well, let me discomfort you. I was *not* pleased to have
you. Get a younger man, I said to him . . .

THE WIFE
Be kind.

THE BEST FRIEND
There are customs . . .

THE DOCTOR
(*Not hurt; not angry; shrugs*)
And you had them . . . the surgeons, the consultants,
younger—well, not brash, but I doubt you'd have
wanted that.

THE WIFE
. . . some bouncy intern with a scalpel in one hand, a
racquet under his arm . . .

THE MISTRESS
(*Mildly annoyed*)
Don't be ridiculous.

THE DOCTOR
(*Chuckles*)

I'm rather like a priest: you have me for the limits, for birth and dying, *and* for the minor cuts and scratches in between. If that nagging cough keeps nagging, now it's not *me* opens up the throat or the chest; not *me*. *I* send you on to *other* men . . . and very quickly. I am the most . . . general of practitioners.

THE MISTRESS

I'm sorry.

THE DOCTOR

'Course, if you think some younger man would do better here, have him back on his feet and at the fireplace, clinking the ice in a bourbon, looking better than ever . . .

THE MISTRESS
(*Wants no more of it*)

No! I *said* I am sorry. Just . . . railing against it.
(*Gently*)

I *am* sorry.

THE BEST FRIEND
(*To* THE MISTRESS, *really; but, to* THE DOCTOR, *and to the others*)

The custom of the house. And it *has* been, for so long. "You end up with what you start out with."

THE WIFE
(*Quiet, choked laughter*)

Oh; God! "The little girl I was when he came to me."

THE MISTRESS
(*After a pause*)
The house? The custom of which house?

THE BEST FRIEND
(*Dogged, not unpleasant*)
Of wherever he is: the house he carries on his back, or in his head.

THE MISTRESS
(*Mildly assertive; slightly bewildered*)
Well . . . I thought I knew it *all:* having been so . . . having participated so fully.

THE WIFE
(*To* THE BEST FRIEND)
Is it written on one of your lovely things? . . . your pieces of paper? That we end up with what we start out with? Or that *he* does?

THE BEST FRIEND
(*Quiet smile*)
No.

THE WIFE
I thought not, for Dr. Dey, who brought him into this world . . . into all this, went down with that boat, ship, rather—the iceberg one, or was it the German sub; the iceberg, I think.

THE SON
Titanic.

THE WIFE

Thank you.

THE NURSE

Dey did not go down with a ship.

THE WIFE *and* THE BEST FRIEND
(*Slightly overlapping, almost simultaneously*)

He did *not?*

THE NURSE
(*To* THE DOCTOR)

May I? . . .

(THE DOCTOR *nods*)

. . . Dey went down with what we all go down with, and one *day,* you will forgive the pun, he realized the burning far too up in the chest, and the sense of the kidneys saying they can not go on, and the sudden knowledge that it has all gone on . . . from what central, possibly stoppable place—like eating that last, un-wanted shard, that salad, breathing that air from the top of . . . where?—that one thing we are born to discover and never find.

(*Pause*)

He focused in on his killer, and he looked on it, and he said, "I will not have you."

(*Pause*)

And so he booked on the Titanic, of *course.*

THE SON
(*Abstracted*)

Well . . . that is what I thought.

THE MISTRESS
(*Sensing something*)

Of course.

THE NURSE
(*Lighter*)

Or something like it. I mean, if the cancer's on you and you're a doctor to boot and know the chances *and* the pain, well . . . what do you do save book on a boat you think's going to run into an iceberg and sink.

THE SON
(*Frowning*)

Oh. Then he did *not* go down on the Titanic.

THE NURSE

No; he went to Maine, to his lodge, and fished . . . for about a week. Then he killed himself.

THE WIFE

And the story of the ship . . .

THE NURSE

. . . was a fiction, invented by his wife and agreed to by his mistress, by the happy coincidence that the Titanic *did* go down when he did. Oh, nobody *believed* it, you understand; the obituaries were candid; but it became a euphemism and was eventually accepted.

THE WIFE

Poor woman.

THE MISTRESS

Poor *women*.

THE WIFE

Who was his mistress? I didn't know he had one.

THE NURSE
(*Casual*)

I was.

THE WIFE

My gracious; you're . . . *old, aren't* you.

THE NURSE

Yes; very.

THE WIFE
(*After the slightest pause*)

It never occurred to me before. You've always been
such a . . . presence. I don't believe a single word
you've told us.

THE NURSE
(*Shrugs*)

I don't care.
(*Returns to her place by the bed.
Pause*)

THE DOCTOR

You see . . .

THE MISTRESS
(*Quite annoyed*)

You *always* say that!

THE WIFE
(*Not sure, but interested*)

Does he?

42

THE DOCTOR

You see, I did my tithe all at once, in the prisons, when I was young. After my internship; I went to help.

THE WIFE

We never knew that.

THE MISTRESS

No.

THE DOCTOR

No?

(*Shrugs, chuckles*)

It was a while ago: it was before our minds had moved to the New Testament, or our reading of it. Men would die, then—for their killings—soon, if . . . well, perhaps not decently, but what passed for decently if burning a man alive survived the test . . . we were all Old Testament Jews, and we still are, two hundred million of us, save the children, for we believe what we no longer practice . . . *if: if* the justice was merciful, for that is what sets us medicine men apart from jurors: we are not in a hurry. But, I was with them; stayed with them; helped them have what they wanted for the last time. I would be with them, and they were alone in the death cells, no access to each other, and the buggery was over, had it ever begun, the buggery and the rest; and there were some, in the final weeks, who had abandoned sex, masturbation, to God, or fear, or some enveloping withdrawal, but not all; some . . . some made love to themselves in a frenzy—indeed, I treated more than one who was bleeding from it, from so much—and several confided to me that their masturbation image was their executioner . . . some fancy of how he looked.

THE WIFE
(*Remembering an announcement*)
The little girl I was when he came to me.

THE DOCTOR
You see:

THE WIFE
(*Laughing a little*)
You see? No one cares.

THE DOCTOR
I . . . am eighty-six . . . which, I was informed by my grandson, or perhaps my great-nephew—I confuse them, not the two, but the . . .
(*Confiding*)
well, they look alike, and have what I confess I think of as wigs, though I know they are not . . .
(*Some, though not fruity, longing here*)
. . . long, lovely . . . turning down and underneath at the shoulders . . . blond and grail-like hair . . . but they said . . . or one of them did . . .
(*Not loud, but emphasized*)
. . . "Eighty-six! Man, that means going out!" Well, of course, I knew what they meant, but I was coy with it—and I asked them why—what does that make me? "Eighty-six and out." Does that make me . . . and suddenly I knew! I knew I wanted to lie in the long blond hair, put my lips there in the back of the neck, with the blond hair over me . . .

THE SON
(*Great urgency*)

I don't *follow* you!

THE DOCTOR

I was completing what I had begun before: how we
become enraptured by it . . .
(*Small smile*)
. . . by the source of our closing down. You see: I
suddenly loved my executioners . . . well, figurative;
and in the way of . . . nestling up against them, hud-
dling close—for we do seek warmth, affection even,
from those who tell us we are going to die, or when.

THE MISTRESS
(*After a pause*)

I believe in the killing; *some* of it; for *some* of them.

THE WIFE

Of *course*. Give us a theory and we'll do it in.

THE BEST FRIEND
(*Quiet distaste*)

You *can't* believe in it.

THE WIFE

See . . . your own wife.

THE BEST FRIEND
(*Gut betrayal, but soft-keyed*)

You *can't* do that. There was no killing there.

THE WIFE

Just . . . divorce. It wasn't *us* that did her in—our . . .

45

late summer . . . arrangement: there had been others. *Our* . . . mercy to each other, by the lake, the city . . . *that* didn't take a wild woman who could still bake bread and give a party half the time and send her spinning back into the animal brain; no, my dear; fucking—as it is called in public by everyone these days—is not what got at her; yours and mine, I mean. Divorce: leave *alone:* So don't tell *me* you don't believe in murder. You *do. I* do.

> (*Indicates* THE MISTRESS)

She does, and admits it.

THE SON
> (*Without moving*)

I WANT TO TALK TO HIM!

THE BEST FRIEND
> (*To* THE WIFE, *quiet; intense*)

You said she was insane. You *all* said it.

THE WIFE
> (*Rather dreamy*)

Did I? Well, perhaps I meant she was *going.*
> (*Enigmatic smile*)

Perhaps we all did.
> (*To* THE SON)

Then talk to him. You can preface every remark by saying "for the first and last time." And you'll get no argument—there's *that.* I'd not *do* it, though.
> (*Dry*)

You'd start to cry; you've little enough emotion in you: I'd save it.

THE SON
(*To his mother; frustration; controlled rage*)
He's *dying!*

THE WIFE
(*Sad; comforting; explaining*)
I *know.*

THE BEST FRIEND
(*Quiet; more or less to himself*)
It was progressive. I *asked* them. The violence was
transitional.
(*To* THE WIFE)
I saw her not two months ago.

THE MISTRESS
(*Seeing that* THE WIFE *is preoccupied*)
Did you!

THE BEST FRIEND
I had been to the club, and was getting in my car;
another pulled up alongside and someone said—coolly,
I think—"Well; I declare." It was a voice I knew,
and I turned my head and it was her sister behind the
wheel, with another woman in the death seat beside
her, as it is called. "I *do* declare," she said—definitely
cool—and I perceived it in an instant, before I looked,
that my wife was in the back, my ex-wife, and the
woman in the front was from the hospital: no uniform,
but an attendant of some sort. "Look who we have
here!" That was the way she talked, the smile set, the
eyes madder than my wife's could ever be—a sane
woman, though. The attendant was smoking, I remember that. Of course I looked, and indeed she *was*

47

there, in the back, catercorner, a fur rug half back-drop, half cocoon, and how small she was in it! "Look who's here," her sister said, this time addressing *her,* her head turned to catch both our expressions. The windows were down and I put my hands on the sill—if that *is* what car doors have—and bent down some. "Hello," I said, "how are you?", realizing as I said it that if she laughed in my face, or screamed, or went for me I would not have been surprised. She smiled, though, and stroked the fur beside her cheek with the back of her hand. Her voice was calm, and extremely . . . rested. "It's fine in here," she said, "how is it out there?" I didn't reply: I was so aware of her eyes on me, and her sister's, and the attendant not turned, but looking straight ahead, and smoking. She went on: "Oh, it would be so nice to say to you, 'Come closer, so I can whisper something to you.' That way I could put my hand to the back of your head and say very softly, 'Help me'; either that or rub my lips against your ear, the way you like, and then *grab* you with my teeth, and hold on as you pulled away, blood, and ripping." It was so . . . ob-jective, and without rancor, I didn't move at all; the attendant did, I remember; she turned. "I can't do that, though," my wife said—sadly, I think. "Do you know why?" "No, I don't know why." "Because," she said, "when I look at your ear I see the rump and the tail of a mouse coming out from it; he must be chewing very deeply." I didn't move; my fingers stayed where they were. It could be I was trying to fashion some reply, but there *is* none to that. Her sister gunned the motor then; having seen me when she parked, she must have thought to keep it idling. "Nice to see you," she said to me, the same grim smile, mad eyes, and she backed out, curving, shifted, and moved off. And what I retain of their leaving, most of all, above the mouse, my wife, *myself,* for that matter, is the sound of her sister's bracelet clanking against the steering wheel—a massive gold chain with a disc suspended from it, a large thin disc, with her first name, in facsimile, scrawled across one face of it; that; clanking as she shifted.

(*Pause*)

THE WIFE
(*Having listened to almost all the story*)
Then I'm sorry.

THE BEST FRIEND
(*Quietly; a little weary*)
It's all right.

(*Pause*)

THE SON
It's not true, you know: there's more emotion in me than you think.

THE WIFE
(*Gentle, placating*)
Well, I hope so.
(*Pause; to* THE MISTRESS)
You're very silent.

THE MISTRESS
I was *wondering* about that: why I *was*. I'd *noticed* it and was rather puzzled. It's not my *way*.

49

THE WIFE
(*Agreeing*)

No.

THE MISTRESS

Outsider, I guess.

THE WIFE
(*Friendly*)

Oh, stop!

THE MISTRESS

No; really; yes. In this context. Listening to you was
a capping on it, I suppose: *God;* that was effective
as you did it, and I dare say you *needed* it. Maybe
that's how we keep the nineteenth century going for
ourselves: pretend it exists, and . . . well . . . outsider.

THE WIFE
(*Objective curiosity, but friendly*)

What will you *do?*

THE MISTRESS
(*Thinks about that for a while*)

I don't *know*. I really don't. Give me a schedule. Who
runs to the coverlet first? And who throws her arms
where, and where, and where does it matter? Who
grabs the shoulders, to shake the death out of them,
and who collapses at the knees?

THE WIFE
(*Not sure, herself*)

You don't *know*.

THE MISTRESS
(*Laughs, so sadly*)

Oh, God, the little girl you were when he came to you.

THE WIFE
(*Sad truth*)

Yes!

THE MISTRESS
(*Sad truth*)

I don't *know*.

   (THE DAUGHTER *enters; her swift opening of
   the door jars them all to quiet attention; she
   chuckles a little, unpleasantly, at their reac-
   tion, and moves to the fireplace without a
   word; she rests her hands on the mantel, and
   stares into the fire*)

Ultimately, an outsider. I was *thinking* about that, and
I concluded it was ritual that made it so.

   (*Looking about; almost amused*)

This is . . . ritual, is it not?

   (*Normal tone*)

Twenty years without it, except an awkwardness at
Christmas, perhaps.

   (*To* THE WIFE)

I remember one December in particular, when it was
in the papers you were suing for divorce. Glad you
didn't, I think; it would have forced him to marry
me . . . or not. Move off.

   (*Generally*)

He missed you all then. Oh, he always *has* . . . mildly,
but *that* Christmas—we were at the lodge; it was the
next year we took to the islands, to avoid the season
as much as anything, though it *was* good for his back,

51

the sun—that one in particular, we sat before the great fire, with all the snow and the pines, and I knew he missed . . . well: family.

(*Small laugh*)

He missed the ritual, I think.

(*Not unkindly*)

I doubt you were very good with Christmas, though; hardly . . . prototypical: wassail, and chestnuts.

THE SON
(*Slightly triste*)

Once. Chestnuts.

THE WIFE
(*To* THE MISTRESS; *a smile*)

You *are* right.

THE MISTRESS

In front of the fire; Christmas Eve. We *had* been holding hands, but were *not;* not at that moment, and did he sigh? Perhaps; but there was a great . . . all of a sudden, a . . . slack, and I caught his profile as he stared into the fire, that . . . marvelous granite, and it was as if he had . . . deflated, just perceptibly. I took his hand, and he turned to me and smiled: came back. I said, "You should spend it with *them;* every *year.*" He said he thought not, and it was not for *my* sake.

THE DAUGHTER
(*Still staring into the fire; she intones the word, spreads it*)

Drone. Drone!

THE MISTRESS

(*Looks up at* THE DAUGHTER*'s back, pauses
a moment, looks out at nothing; continues*)

It *is* the ritual, you see, that gives me the sense. The
first few times I wouldn't go to his doctorates, until
he *made* me do it, and the banquets when he *spoke!*
Naturally, I've never thought of myself as a secret—
for I am not a tart, and I would never have been
good at it—but the rituals remind me of what I believe
is called my . . . status. To be something so fully, and
yet . . . well, no matter.

(*A quick, bright laugh; the next directed to*
THE WIFE)

I wonder: if I had been *you*—the little girl you were
when he came to you—would you have come along,
as I did? Would *you* have come to take *my* place?

THE DAUGHTER

(*As* THE WIFE *is about to speak; turns, but
stays at the fireplace*)

They're all down there! The cameramen, the television
crews, the reporters. They gave me a container of
coffee.

THE WIFE

Well, why aren't they being *looked* after? Didn't you
tell them in the kitchen to see what was needed,
and . . .

THE DAUGHTER

The ones out*side*: the crews with their trucks and
lights. *They* gave me the coffee.

(*Laughs, but it is not pleasant*)

It's like a *fungus*. The TV people are on the stoop,

with all their equipment on the sidewalk, and you and
your tubes and wires! Like a fungus: all of those
outside, and the photographers have assumed the en-
trance hall, like a stag line—nobody sits!, and the
newspapermen have taken the library, for that is where
the Scotch is.

THE WIFE
(*To* THE BEST FRIEND)
Go down and *do* something!

THE DAUGHTER
(*It is clear she's enjoying it, in a sad way*)
Don't bother! It's all been set. Touch it and you'll
have it on the landing. Leave it.
(*Looks toward her father's bed; overplayed*)
Who *is* this man?

THE WIFE
(*Trailing off*)
Well, I suppose . . .

THE DAUGHTER
I forgot to mention the police.

THE WIFE
(*Mild anxiety*)
The police!

THE DAUGHTER
(*Very much "on"*)
For the people. Well, there aren't many there now,
people, twenty-five, maybe—the kind of crowd you'd

get for a horse with sunstroke, if it were summer. The TV has brought them out, the trucks and the tubes. They're lounging, nothing better to do, and if it weren't night and a weekend, I doubt they'd linger. I mean, God, we don't have the President in here, or anything.

THE SON
(*Quiet, but dismayed*)
Don't talk like that.

THE WIFE
(*To* THE BEST FRIEND)
Shouldn't you go down?

THE BEST FRIEND
(*Shakes his head*)
No; it's a public event; *will* be.

THE NURSE
That's the final test of fame, isn't it, the degree of it: which is newsworthy, the act of dying itself, or merely the death.

THE MISTRESS
(*Aghast*)
MERELY!

THE NURSE
(*Almost a reproach*)
I wasn't speaking for me, *or* you. *Them.* The public; whether it's enough for them to read about it in the papers without a kind of anger at having missed the dying, too. They were cheated with the Kennedys, both

of them, *and* with King. It happened so fast; all people could figure for themselves was they'd been clubbed in the face by history. Even poor Bobby; he took the longest, but everybody knew he was dead before he died. Christ, that loathsome doctor on the tube kept telling us.

(*Imitation of a person despised*)

"There's no chance at *all* as I see it; the hemorrhaging, the bullet where it is. No chance. No chance." Jesus, you couldn't even *hope*. It was a disgusting night; it made me want to be young, and a man, and violent and unreasoning—rage so that it meant something. Pope John was the last one the public could share in—two weeks of the vilest agony, and conscious to the very end, unsedated, because it was something his God wanted him to experience. I don't know, maybe a bullet *is* better. In spite of everything.

THE WIFE

Perhaps.

THE MISTRESS
(*Quiet sadness*)

What a sad and shabby time we live in.

THE WIFE

Yes.

THE DAUGHTER
(*Begins to laugh; incredulous, cruel*)

You . . . hypocrites!

THE WIFE

Oh?

56

THE DAUGHTER

You pious hypocrites!

(*Mocking*)

The sad and shabby time we live in. "Yes." You dare to sit there and shake your heads like that!?

(*To* THE WIFE)

To hell with you with your . . . affair with him, though that's not bad for sad and shabby, *is* it.

(*Points to* THE MISTRESS)

But what about *her!*

THE WIFE
(*Curious*)

What *about* her?

THE MISTRESS
(*She, too*)

Yes; what *about* me?

THE DAUGHTER

Mistress is a pretty generous term for what it's all about, isn't it? So is *kept*. Isn't that *another* euphemism? And how much do you think she's gotten from him? Half a million? A million?

THE MISTRESS

There are things you do *not* know, little girl.

THE WIFE
(*Steel*)

You live with a man who will not divorce his wife, who has become a drunkard because of him, and who is doubtless supplied with her liquor gratis from *his liquor* store—a business which is, I take it, the height of his ambition—who has taken more money from you than I like to think about, who has broken one rib that I know of, and blackened your eyes, and has *dared . . . dared* to come to me and suggest I intercede with your father . . .

THE DAUGHTER
(*Furious*)

ALL RIGHT!

THE WIFE

. . . in a political matter which *stank* of the Mafia . . .

THE DAUGHTER
(*A scream*)

ALL RIGHT!

THE WIFE
(*A change of tone to loss*)

You know a lot about sad and shabby; you know far too much to turn the phrase on others, especially on those who do *not* make a point of doing what they will or must as badly as possible. That is probably what I have come to love you so little for—that *you* love yourself so little. Don't ever tell *me* to make a life, or *anyone* who does things out of love, or even affection.

(*Pause*)

You were beautiful, you know. You really were. Once.
(THE DAUGHTER *opens her mouth as if to respond; thinks otherwise; moves away.*
Silence as they think on this)

58

THE MISTRESS
(*Some delight; really to bring them all back*)
My parents are both still alive—I suddenly remember.
They are neither . . . particularly *limber,* they keep to
themselves more than not, and my father's eyesight is
such that when he dares to drive at all it is down the
center lines of the road. Oh, it makes the other drivers
cautious. She's learned that snapping at him does no
good at all, and the one time she put her hand on the
wheel, thinking—she told me later—that his drift to
the left was becoming more pronounced than ever, he
resisted her, and the result was weaving, and horns,
and a ditch, or shoulder, whichever it is, and a good
deal of heavy breathing.

THE BEST FRIEND
Why doesn't *she* drive?

THE MISTRESS
(*Smiles a little*)
No; she could learn, but I imagine she'd rather sit
there with him and see things his way.

THE DAUGHTER
(*Dry*)
Why doesn't she walk, or take a taxi, or just not go?

THE MISTRESS
(*Knows she is being mocked, but prefers to
teach rather than hit back*)
Oh; she loves him, you see.
(*Laughs again*)
My *grand*father died only last *year.*

THE DAUGHTER
(*Spat out*)

Oh, *stop* it!

THE MISTRESS
(*Controlled*)

Please stop telling me to stop it.
(*Generally*)

He was a hundred and three, my mother's father, and he was not at all like those centenarians you're always reading about: full head of snow-white hair, out chopping wood all the time when they weren't burying their fourth wife or doing something worthy in the Amazon; not a bit of it. He was a wispy little man, whom none of us liked very much—not even my mother, who would be a saint one day, were it not for Luther; a tiny man, with the face of a starving child, and blond hair of the type that white does not become, and very little of that, and bones, it would appear, of the finest porcelain, for he fell, when he was seventy-two, and did to his pelvis what you would do to a teapot were you to drop it on a flagstone floor.

THE DOCTOR
(*Factual; nothing else*)

The bones dry out.

THE MISTRESS

Indeed they must, for he took to his bed—or was taken there—and remained in it for thirty-one years. He wanted to be read to a lot.

THE WIFE
(*She tries to get the two words out sensibly, but breaks up during it into a helpless laugh-*

60

*ter; she covers her mouth, and her eyes dart
from person to person; the words are:)*

Poor man!

*(Finally she quiets herself, but a glance at
her daughter staring at her with distaste sends
her into another outburst; this one she controls rather more easily)*

THE MISTRESS

*(After the second outburst has quieted; very
serious)*

Shh, now. As I said, he wanted to be read to a lot.

*(THE WIFE smothers giggles occasionally dur-
ing this)*

This was not easy for his family and fast-diminishing
set of friends, for he was hard of hearing and one
had to shout;

(She holds her right index finger up)

plus; plus, everyone knew he had the eyesight of a
turkey buzzard.

*(THE BEST FRIEND starts to giggle a bit, too,
now)*

THE DAUGHTER

Stop it!

THE MISTRESS

So, finally, of course, one had to start hiring people.

THE DAUGHTER
(As THE WIFE laughs)

Stop it!

61

THE WIFE
(*She can no longer control her hysteria*)
A turkey-buzzard!?
(*Her newest explosion of laughter is enough to set* THE SON *off as well, and, to a lesser degree,* THE DOCTOR *and* THE NURSE)

THE DAUGHTER
Stop it!

THE WIFE
It's not *true, is* it!

THE MISTRESS
(*As she breaks up, herself*)
No; not a word of it!
(*Note: While this laughter should have the look, to those who have watched it, and the feel, to those who have experienced it, of the self-generating laughter possible under marijuana, we should be aware that it is, in truth, produced by extreme tension, fatigue, ultimate sadness and existentialist awareness: in other words . . . the reason we always react that way.*
Further note: The ones who have laughed least freely should stop most precipitously, though THE SON *might keep his mirth awhile longer than most.* THE WIFE *and* THE MISTRESS *have an arm around one another*)

THE DAUGHTER
(*She has been saying, "Stop it, stop it; stop it, you fucking bitches!" all through the ulti-*

mate laughter, mostly to THE WIFE *and* THE
MISTRESS, *but at* THE SON, THE NURSE, THE
BEST FRIEND *and* THE DOCTOR *as well.
Clearly, she has meant it for them all, for,
as they stop, not without a whoop or two at
her from time to time, her volume stays
constant, so that, finally, hers is the voice we
hear, and hers only*)

Stop it; stop it; stop it, you bitches, you filthy . . .
you filth who allow it . . . you . . . you . . .
(*Stop*)

THE WIFE
(*She is the one who stops first, becomes fixed
on* THE DAUGHTER)

You! *You* stop it!

THE DAUGHTER

You bitches! You fucking . . .
(*Stops; realizes*)

THE WIFE
(*A quiet, post-hysterical smile*)

Why don't you go home to your *own* filth? You . . .
you . . . issue!
(*Sits back, eyes her coldly*)

THE DAUGHTER
(*Rage only, now*)

Your morality is . . . it's incredible; it really is; it's a
model for the world. You're smug, and excluding.
You're incredible! All of you!

THE WIFE
(*Calm; seemingly detached*)

Well, since you've nothing else to do, why don't you run downstairs and tell the waiting press about . . . *our* morality? And while you're at it . . . tell them about your own as well.

THE DAUGHTER
(*So intense she can barely get it through her teeth*)

This woman has come and taken . . . my . . . *father!*

THE WIFE
(*After a pause; not sad; a little weary; empty, perhaps*)

Yes. My *hus*band. Remember?
(*Sighs*)

And that makes all the difference. Perhaps your fancy man has people who care for him, who worry after him; they are not my concern. They may be *yours,* but I doubt it. *I* . . . *care;* about what happens *here.* This woman loves my husband—as *I* do—and she has made him happy; as *I* have. She is good, and decent, and she is not moved by envy and self-loathing . . .

THE DAUGHTER
(*Close to rage again*)

. . . like some people?!! . . .

THE WIFE

. . . Indeed. Like *some* people.

THE DAUGHTER
(*A stuck record*)

Like *you!?* Like *you!?* Like *you!?*

THE WIFE
(*Shuts her eyes for a moment, as if to shut out the sound*)
Somewhere, in the rubble you've made of your life so far, you must have an instinct tells you why she's part of us. No? She *loves* us. And we love *her*.

THE DAUGHTER
(*A rough, deep voice*)
Do *you* love *me*?
(*Pause; her tone becomes fiercer*)
Does *anyone* love me?

THE WIFE
(*A bright little half-caught laugh escapes her; her tone instantly becomes serious*)
Do *you* love anyone?
(*A silence.*
THE DAUGHTER *stands for a moment, swaying, quivering just perceptibly; then she turns on her heel, opens the door and slams it behind her*)

THE BEST FRIEND
(*As* THE WIFE *sighs, reaches for* THE MISTRESS' *hand*)
Will she? Will she go down and tell the waiting press?

THE WIFE
(*True curiosity*)
I don't *know*. I don't think she would; but I don't *know*.
(*Laughs as she did before*)
I laughed before, because it was so unlikely. I had an

65

aunt, a moody lady, but with cause. She died when she was twenty-six—died in the heart, that is, or whatever portion of the brain controls the spirit; she went on, all the appearances, was snuffed out, finally, at sixty-two, in a car crash, all done up in jodhpurs and a derby, yellow scarf with the foxhead stickpin, driving in the vintage car, the old silver touring car, the convertible with the window between the front and back seats, back from the stable, from jumping, curved, bashed straight into the bread truck, Parkerhouse rolls and blood, her twenty-six-year heart emptying out of her sixty-two-year body, on the foxhead pin and the metal and the gasoline, and all the cardboard boxes sprawled on the country road.

(*Slight pause*)

"Does anyone love me?" she asked, once, back when I was nine, or ten. There were several of us in the room, but they were used to it. "Do *you* love anyone?" I asked her back. Slap! Then tears—hers *and* mine; mine not from the pain but the . . . effrontery; hers . . . both; effrontery *and* pain.

THE MISTRESS
(*After a short silence*)

Hmmmm. Yes.

(*The door bursts open, and* THE DAUGHTER *catapults into the room, leaving the door wide*)

THE DAUGHTER

YOU tell them!

(TWO PHOTOGRAPHERS *and* A REPORTER *enter tentatively; in the moment it takes for the*

*people assembled to react, they have moved
a step or two in.*
Then the room moves into action. THE DOC-
TOR *and* THE NURSE *stay where they are, but
transfixed;* THE SON *rises from his chair;* THE
BEST FRIEND *takes a step or two forward;*
THE WIFE *and* THE MISTRESS *rise, poised*)

THE BEST FRIEND

Get back downstairs; you can't come . . .
(But it is THE WIFE *and* THE MISTRESS *who
move*)

THE WIFE
(A beast's voice, really)

Get . . . out . . . of . . . here!
*(The two women attack, fall upon the in-
truders with fists and feet, and there is an
animal fury within them which magnifies
their strength. The struggle is brief, but intense; one of the cameramen has his camera
knocked to the floor, where he leaves it as
the three men retreat.* THE WIFE *forces the
door shut, turns, leans against it.* THE
DAUGHTER *has her back to the audience,
with* THE WIFE *and* THE MISTRESS *to either
side of her, facing her. No words; heavy
breathing; almost a tableau.*
Finally; it is an animal's sound; rage, pain)
AARRRGGGHHH.
(Two seconds silence)

CURTAIN

ACT TWO

*The scene: the same as before, fifteen min-
utes later.* THE DOCTOR *and* THE NURSE *are
at the bed, half asleep on their feet, or perhaps* THE DOCTOR *has fallen asleep on a
chair near the bed.* THE BEST FRIEND *is by
the fireplace, gazing into it;* THE WIFE *is dozing in a chair;* THE MISTRESS *is in a chair
near the fireplace;* THE DAUGHTER *is in a
chair somewhat removed from the others,
facing front;* THE SON *is massaging her
shoulders.*
*It seems very late: the exhaustion has over-
whelmed them; even awake they seem to be
in a dream state. What one says is not picked
up at once by another.*

71

THE SON
(*Gently*)

You shouldn't have done that. You know you shouldn't.

THE DAUGHTER
(*Really not anxious to talk about it*)
I know I shouldn't. Gentler.

THE SON

No matter how you feel.

THE DAUGHTER

I *know*. I *said* I *know*.

THE SON

If they'd gotten in . . .

THE DAUGHTER

Not with our sentries; you'd need an army for that.

THE SON

No matter *how* you feel.

THE DAUGHTER
(*Languid*)

I feel . . . well, how you must have felt when you were young, at school, and you'd fail, or be dismissed, to make some point you didn't know quite what. Like that.
(*Quite without emotion*)
I feel like a child, rebellious, misunderstood and known oh, so very well; sated and . . . empty. I'm *on* to myself; there's no mistake there. I'm all the things you

think of me, every one of you, and I'm also many more.

(*An afterthought*)

I wonder why they didn't kill me, the two of them.

THE SON

There's enough death going here.

THE DAUGHTER

Oh, I don't know. God knows, I can probably go my own way now, without a word or a look from any of you. Non grata *has* its compensations. Go my own way. What a relief.

(*Ironic*)

Back to that "degradation" of mine. Imagine her!, degrading a family as famous as this, up by its own boot straps—well, the only one of it who mattered, anyway—all the responsibility to itself, the Puritan moral soul. How does it go?: "Since we have become what we are, then the double edge is on us; we cannot back down, for we are no longer private, and the world has its eye on us." Christ, you'd think we were only nominally mortal, *he* at any rate; he's the only one who matters, and *he's* mortal enough, is going to prove to be. And the eye of the world! Eyes are attached to the brain, I believe, and the monster is sluggish nowadays, all confused and retreating, surly but withdrawn. *Folk* heroes, maybe, but not *his* type, too much up *here*. If you can't take it in all at once—relate to it, dear God—grant it its due, but don't dwell on it. The dust bin; anachronism. Well, I'll be glad when he's gone—no, no, not for the horrid reasons, not for all of your mistakes about me, but simply that the tintype can be thrown away, the sturdy group, and I can be what I choose to be with only half of the disapproval, no longer the public. *You* won't get in the press because you're someone's son, unless you get arrested for something serious, *or* newsworthy. Nor will I. I'll have my man—such as he is and such as I want him for—and only mother will really mind. We'll see each other less, all of us, and finally not at all, I'd imagine—except on . . . occasions. Whatever we disdain will be our own affair. You can, too, probably, very soon . . . when all *this* is finished.

THE SON

Do *what.*

THE DAUGHTER

Resign . . . You'll be rich enough, or do you want to go on with it, even when he's gone? Isn't it pointless for you there? Aren't you useless?

THE SON
(Wry little laugh)

Probably. I don't like it very much; I don't feel *part* of it, though it's a way of getting through from ten to six, and avoiding all I know I'd be doing if I didn't have it . . .

(Smiles a bit)

those demons of mine.

THE DAUGHTER
(Laughs a little)

Ah, those demons. You're no different.

(Turns toward THE BEST FRIEND)

Will you keep him on—

74

(Mildly mocking)

at the *firm*—after . . . all this is finished, and you've no more obligation to our father, or did you make a bond to keep it up forever?

THE BEST FRIEND
(Quietly)

There's no bond; your brother isn't with me as a charity.

(To THE SON)

You don't think that, do you? You fill your position nicely and you're nicely paid for doing it. If you choose to leave, of course, nothing will falter, nor, for that matter, will I feel any . . . particular loss, but we know that about each other, don't we. But no one's waiting to throw you down. That's your sister's manner.

(To THE DAUGHTER)

Don't ask me to talk about it now.

THE SON
(To THE BEST FRIEND; very simple)

I didn't know that you didn't care for me. I suppose I always assumed . . . well, that we were all a form of family, and . . .

(Shrugs)

THE DAUGHTER
(Sad advice)

Don't assume.

THE SON

Well; no matter.

THE BEST FRIEND
(*A little impatient*)

Did I say I didn't *care* for you? I thought I said I'd
feel no loss if you were gone. I'm pretty much out of
loss.

(*He turns back to the fire*)

THE SON

Sorry; that *is* what you said.

(*To* THE DAUGHTER)

Enough? More?

THE DAUGHTER

The base of the neck, and slowly, very slowly. Uh
hunh.

(*Sensuous, as he massages her neck*)

They were animals, and I had a moment of . . . absolutely thrilling dread, very much as when I read of
the Chinese, and how they are adept at keeping a
man alive and conscious, *conscious,* for hours, while
they strip the skin from his body. They tie him to a
pole.

THE SON

What for?

THE DAUGHTER

So he won't wander off, I'd imagine. I'm not your
usual masochist, in spite of what *she* thinks. I mean,
a broken rib really *hurts,* and everybody over twelve
knows what a black eye on a lady *means.* I don't

fancy any of that, but I do care an awful lot about the guilt I can produce in those that do the hurting.
(*Suddenly a little girl*)
Mother?

THE SON

She's sleeping.

THE DAUGHTER
(*Turns to* THE MISTRESS)
You're not.

THE MISTRESS
(*Coming back*)

Hm?

THE DAUGHTER
You're not, *are* you. Sleeping.

THE MISTRESS
(*Not hostile; still half away*)
No. I'm far too exhausted.

THE DAUGHTER
(*To* THE SON; *plaintive*)
Wake mother up.

THE BEST FRIEND
(*Sotto voce*)
Let her sleep, for God's sake!

THE MISTRESS
(*Voice low; cool*)
Do you want to start in again? Do you have some new pleasure for us?

THE DAUGHTER
(*Heavy sigh*)
I want to tell her that I'm sorry.

THE MISTRESS
I dare say she knows that; has, for years.

THE DAUGHTER
Still . . .

THE MISTRESS
Nobody's a fool here.

THE DAUGHTER
(*Mildly biting*)
You were never a mother.

THE MISTRESS
(*Smiles*)
No, nor have you been, but you've been a woman.

THE DAUGHTER
(*Ironic*)
And the old instinct's always there, right?

THE MISTRESS
Right.

THE DAUGHTER
But you have been a wife, haven't you, twice as I
remember, not to count your adventures in mistress-
hood. How many men have you gone through, hunh?
No divorces, you; just bury them.

THE MISTRESS
(*Calm, but intent*)
Listen to me, young lady, there are things you have
no idea of, matters might cross your mind were you
not so . . . self-possessed. You lash out—which can
be a virtue, I dare say, stridency aside, if it's used to
protect and not just as a revenge . . .

THE DAUGHTER
(*To cut it off*)
O.K. O.K.

THE MISTRESS
. . . but you're careless, not only with facts, but of
your*self*. What words will you ever have left if you
use them all to kill? What words will you summon up
when the day *comes,* as it may, poor you, when you
suddenly discover that you've been in love—oh, for a
week, say, and not known it, not having been familiar
with the symptoms, being such an amateur? Love with
mercy, I mean, the kind you can't hold back as a
reward, or use as any sort of weapon. What vocabulary
will you have for that? Perhaps you'll be mute; many
are—the self-conscious—in a foreign land, with only
the phrases the guidebook gives them, or maybe it will
be dreamlike for you—nightmarish—lockjawed, throat
constricted, knowing that whatever word you use,
whatever phrase you might say will come out, not as
you mean it then, but as you have meant before, that
"I love you; I need you," no matter how joyously
meant, will be the snarl of a wounded and wounding
animal. You'd better go back to grade school.

THE DAUGHTER
(*Contempt and self-disgust*)
Oh, I'm far too old for that, aren't I?

THE MISTRESS
(*Shrugs*)
Perhaps you are. It would serve you right.

THE DAUGHTER
There's ignorance enough in you, too, you know.
You've not been that much in touch—except with *him*,
and he's hardly one to keep up to date.

THE MISTRESS
So true. But—and I *do* hate to say it, I really do—
unless you're some kind of unique, I've seen your
type before.

THE DAUGHTER
(*Quietly*)
Fuck yourself.
(*To* THE SON)
You've stopped.

THE SON
(*Not starting again*)
Yes. My fingers ache.

THE DAUGHTER
(*Quietly, without emotion*)
You never were much good at anything.

THE MISTRESS
(*To* THE BEST FRIEND; *mock ingenuous*)
How am I supposed to do that, I wonder?

THE BEST FRIEND
(*Dry, weary*)

It's usually said to men, but even there it's a figure of speech.

(*He shakes his head, turns back to the fire*)

Don't involve me; please.

(THE DOCTOR *has moved toward them; he stands for a moment*)

THE DOCTOR
(*Quietly*)

That's very interesting; it *is*.

THE SON
(*Soft, but frightened*)

What is?

THE DOCTOR

His heart stopped beating . . . for three beats. Then it started again.

THE DAUGHTER
(*To* THE SON; *anxious*)

Wake mother!

THE DOCTOR
(*With a gesture*)

No; no; it *began* again.

THE DAUGHTER

Maybe you were asleep; you're old enough.

THE DOCTOR

Surely, but I wasn't. Fall asleep with the stethoscope

to his chest, dream of stop and go? Wake immediately, jolted back by the content? No. His heart stopped beating . . . for three beats. Then it started again. Nothing less than that. I thought I'd report it.
            (*He starts to turn back; re-turns*)
It's interesting when it happens, but it's nothing to write home about. Just thought I'd report it, that's all.

THE MISTRESS

What does it signify? It must, something.

THE DOCTOR
(*Thinks, shrugs*)
Weakening. What did you mean, something conscious like fighting it off?

THE MISTRESS
(*Wistful*)

Maybe.

THE DOCTOR
(*Gentle; a smile*)
Nooooo. You're better than that.
            (*He moves back whence he came*)

THE DAUGHTER

They tell you more on television.
            (THE MISTRESS *laughs a little*)
They do!

THE MISTRESS

In a way.

82

THE SON
(*Sober*)
Just think: it could have been finished then.
(*Quickly*)
I don't mean anything but the wonder of it.

THE MISTRESS
(*Dry*)
Why, don't you believe in suffering?

THE DAUGHTER
Does he know he is? Suffering?

THE MISTRESS
I didn't mean him.
(*Refers first to* THE DAUGHTER, *then* THE SON)
I meant you . . . and you. I *do:* believe in suffering.

THE DAUGHTER
(*Quiet scorn*)
What *are* you, a fundamentalist, one of those "God designed it so it must be right" persons, down deep beneath the silvery surface?

THE SON
She didn't mean that.

THE DAUGHTER
(*Ibid.*)
How would *you* know? You're not much good at anything.

THE SON
(*To* THE MISTRESS)
Did you? *Mean* that?

THE MISTRESS

I meant at least two things, as I usually do.
(*To* THE DAUGHTER)
No divorces, I just bury them? Well, what would you
have me do? I know, you meant it as a way of speaking; you were trying to be unkind, but keep it in mind
should your lover be rid of his wife, marry you, and
die. You've been a woman, but you haven't been a
wife. It isn't very nice, you know, to get it all at once—
for both my deaths were sudden: heart attack, and car.
(*Sighs, almost begins to laugh*)
Well, maybe it's better than . . .
(*Indicates the room with a general gesture*)
this. It's all done at once, and you're empty; you go
from that to grief without the intervening pain. You
can't suffer with a man because he's dead; his dying,
yes. The only horror in participating is . . .
(*Thinks better of it*)
. . . well, another time.
(*Pause; shift of tone*)
Look here! You accused me before of being—what is
that old-fashioned word?—a gold digger, of having in-
sinuated myself into . . .

THE DAUGHTER

I said you *probably!*

THE MISTRESS

Yes, of course, but you're imprecise and I know what
you meant. That I am expecting something less than
I have received from your father—money, in other
words, a portion of what you are expecting for having
permitted yourselves to be born.

> (*Turns to* THE BEST FRIEND, *takes his hand;
> he still stares into the fire*)

May I engage you?

> (THE BEST FRIEND *shakes his head, leaves his
> hand where it is; she removes hers*)

No? All right.

> (*Back to* THE DAUGHTER)

You will see, in good time.

> (*Laughs*)

I remember a family once, two children, both well into their fifties, with a dying mother, eighty-something. These children—and there is no allegory here; read yourselves in if you want, but I hope not—these elderly children didn't like each other very much; the daughter had married perhaps not wisely for her second time— penniless, much younger than she, rather fruity to the eye and ear, but perhaps more of a man than most, you never know—but the reasons went further back, the dislike, to some genesis I came upon them too late for, and in the last months of their mother's life they did battle for a percentage of her will, for her estate. But fifty-fifty wouldn't do, and it would shift from that to sixty-forty—seventy-thirty once, I'm told! The mother, you see, had loved them both, and either one who came to her would tilt the balance. But she ended it exactly where she'd started it—half to each— and all that had happened was damage. The daughter was the one at fault, or more grievously, for she had been spoiled in a way that sons are seldom. But all of this is to tell you that I'm not an intruder in the dollar sense. I've more than enough—I was born with it. Don't you people ever take the trouble to scout? And I told your father I wanted nothing beyond his company . . . *and* love. He agreed with me, you'll be distressed to know, said you *needed* it. So. I am not your platinum blonde with the chewing gum and the sequined dress.

THE DAUGHTER
(*After a pause*)

I'm supposed to like you now, I take it, fall into your arms and cry a little and choke out words like sorry and forgive. Well, you've got the wrong lady.

THE MISTRESS
(*Light*)

I wouldn't expect it, and I really don't much care. I've more important things.
(*Less light*)

He taught me a sense of values, you know, beyond what I'd thought was adequate. Cold, I suppose, but right on the button. Took a little while, but I guess I knew I'd go through this someday; so I learned. And you know something else? I'll be there at the funeral, ashes if I have my way—if *he* has *his*—but either way. It's one . . . ritual I'll not defer for.

THE DAUGHTER

You wouldn't dare!

THE MISTRESS

You don't know me, child.

THE DAUGHTER

I won't *have* it.

86

THE SON
(*Gently*)

Be calm.

THE MISTRESS
(*Laughs a little*)

It's not a mind gone mad with power, or a dip into
impropriety, or the need to reopen a wound—for the
wound *is* closed, you know, your mother knows; *you*
do, too; you're railing because you never saw it open;
you can't even find a scar; you don't know where it
was; that *must* be infuriating—none of those things,
but simply that I'll not be put down by sham, and
I'll *be* there, dressed in my gray and white, a friend
of the family. There'll be none of your Italian melo-
drama, with all the buzz as to who is that stranger
off to one side, that woman in black whom nobody
knows, wailing louder than the widow and the family
put together. None of that. I have always known my
place, and I shall know it then. Don't wake her. Let
her sleep.

THE DAUGHTER
(*As* THE NURSE *approaches, tapping a
cigarette*)

You're right: I *am* an amateur.

THE NURSE

May I join you?
(*Nobody replies; she eases into a chair,
clearly exhausted. She lights her cigarette,
inhales, exhales with a great, slow breath*)

Sensible shoes help, but when you're well up into the

'teens, like me, there's nothing for it but this, sometimes.

THE MISTRESS
(*Looking away*)

Any change?

THE NURSE

No; none. Well, of course, some. Procession, but noth-
ing, really.
(*Looks at* THE SON)
You're much too fat; heavy, rather.

THE SON
(*Matter-of-fact*)

I'm sedentary.

THE NURSE

Eat less; do isometrics. You won't last out your fifties.

THE SON
(*Quiet; an echo of something*)

Maybe not?

THE NURSE

Well, I'm not skin and bones, myself, but it's different
for a woman: our hearts are better. Eat fish and raw
vegetables and fruit; avoid everything you like.
(*An afterthought*)
Except sex; have a lot of that: fish, raw vegetables,
fruit and sex.

THE SON
(*Embarrassed*)

Th-thank you.

THE NURSE
Eggs, red flesh, milk-cheese-butter, nuts, most starches
'cept potatoes and rice . . . all bad for you; ignore
them. Two whiskies before dinner, a glass of good
burgundy *with* it, and sex before you go to sleep.
That'll do the trick, keep you going.

THE SON
For?

THE NURSE
(*Rather surprised at his question*)
Until it's proper time for you to die. No point in rush-
ing it.

THE DAUGHTER
(*Eyes upward, head rolling from side to side;
through her teeth*)
Death; death; death; death; death . . .

THE NURSE
(*Taking a drag on her cigarette*)
Death, yes; well, it gets us where we live, doesn't it.
(*A sound startles them. It comes from* THE
WIFE; *it is a sharp, exhaled "Ha-ah." The
first one comes while she is still asleep in her
chair. She bolts upright and awake. She does
it again: "Ha-ah"*)

THE WIFE
(*Fully awake, but still a trifle bewildered*)
I was *asleep*. I *was* asleep. I was dreaming, and I
dreamt I was asleep, and it wakened me. Have—have
I . . . is every—every . . .

89

THE NURSE

It's all right; go back to sleep.

THE WIFE

No, I mustn't; I can't.
(*She rises, a little unsteady, and begins to move toward* THE DOCTOR)
Is everything all right,, is . . .

THE DOCTOR

Everything is all right. Really.
(THE WIFE *moves toward the grouping, sees* THE DAUGHTER, *pauses, eyes her with cold loathing, moves to* THE MISTRESS *and* THE BEST FRIEND, *puts a hand absently on* THE MISTRESS' *shoulder, looks at* THE BEST FRIEND'*s back, then at* THE NURSE)

THE WIFE

(*To* THE NURSE; *no reproach*)
Shouldn't you be back there?

THE NURSE

(*Smiles*)
If I should be, I would be.

THE WIFE

Yes; I'm sorry.
(*Generally; to no one, really*)
I was dreaming of so many things, odd and . . . well, that I was shopping, for a kind of thread, a brand that isn't manufactured any more, and I knew it, but I thought that they might have some in the back. I

couldn't remember the name of the maker, and of course that didn't help. They showed me several that were very much like it, one in particular that I almost settled on, but didn't. They tried to be helpful; it was what they used to call a dry goods store, and it was called that, and I remember a specific . . . not smell, but scent the place had, one that I only remember from being little, so I was clearly in the past, and when they couldn't help, I asked if I could go in the back, the stock. They smiled and said of course, and so I went through a muslin curtain, into the stock, and it was not at all what I'd expected—shelves of cardboard boxes, bales of twine, bolts of fabric, some of the boxes with labels, some with buttons pasted to the end, telling what was there—none of it; it was all canned fruit, and vegetables, peas and carrots and string beans and waxed beans, and bottles of chili sauce and catsup, and canned meats, and everything else I'd not expected and was not a help to me. So I walked back through the muslin and into the living room my family'd had when I was twelve or so, a year before we moved. It was the room my aunt had slapped me in, and I sensed that I was asleep, and it woke me.

THE SON
(*Moves toward a door beside the fireplace, upstage*)
Excuse me.

THE MISTRESS
(*Wistful*)
Dreams.

THE WIFE
(*A little sad*)

Yes.

(THE SON *closes the door behind him.* THE
WIFE *turns to* THE BEST FRIEND)

Are you all right?

THE BEST FRIEND
(*Straightens up, turns, finally, sighs*)

I suppose. Trying to shut it all out helps. I felt a rush
of outrage—back awhile—not over what *she* brought
on,

(*Indicating* THE DAUGHTER)

or my wife's sister, or *myself*, for that matter, or

(*Indicates generally*)

. . . all this, but very generally, as if my brain was going
to vomit, and I thought that if I was very still—as I was
when I was a child, and felt I was about to be sick over
something—it would go away. Well, no, not go away,
but . . . recede.

(*Smiles, sadly*)

It has, I think; some.

THE DAUGHTER
(*Shy, tentative*)

Mother?

THE WIFE

(*Tiniest pause, to indicate she has heard;
speaks to* THE BEST FRIEND)

I upset you, then. I'm sorry; what I said wasn't kind.
You *do* understand it as well as the next.

THE DAUGHTER
(Still pleading quietly, but with an edge to it)
Mo-ther.

THE WIFE
(As before)
And *excluding* you was never my intention, for any
cruel reason, that is. Oh, I may have wanted to join
the two of us together
(Indicates THE MISTRESS*)*
as close as we were but had not admitted, or discussed,
certainly, for we have so much to learn from each
other . . .

THE DAUGHTER
(A growl of frustration and growing anger)
Mooootherrrr!

THE BEST FRIEND
You'd better answer her: she'll go downstairs again.

THE WIFE
(Calm, smiling a little)
No; she's done that once and won't succeed with it
again, for no reason other than you wouldn't let her
out the door . . . would you.
(Pause, as THE BEST FRIEND *winces, smiles
sadly)*
Besides, it wouldn't be shocking any more, merely tire-
some; she'd be pounding her fists on the wind.

THE DAUGHTER
*(Bolt upright in her chair, hands grasping
the arms, neck tendons tight; a howl)*
MOOOOTHERRRRR!!

THE MISTRESS
(*After a pause; gently*)
Do answer her.

THE WIFE
(*Pats* THE MISTRESS *gently on the shoulder;
looks at* THE DAUGHTER; *speaks wistfully, eyes
always on her*)
I may never speak to her again. I'm not certain now—
I have other things on my mind—but there's a good
chance of it: I seldom speak to strangers, and if one
should try to be familiar at a time of crisis, or sorrow,
I'd be enraged.
(*Talks to* THE MISTRESS *now*)
Well, I suppose were I to stumble on the way to the
gravesite and one—she—were to take my elbow to keep
me from falling, I might say thank you, looking straight
ahead. Unlikely, though, isn't it . . . stumbling.
(*Small smile; quietly triumphant*)
No; I don't think I shall speak to her again.
(THE DAUGHTER *rises;* THE WIFE *and* THE MIS-
TRESS *watch.* THE DAUGHTER *seems drained
and very tired; she stands for a moment,
then slowly moves to the upstage chair or
sofa recently abandoned by* THE WIFE; *she
throws herself down on it, turns over on her
back, puts one arm over her eyes, is still.
Softly*)
So much for that.
(*Directly to* THE MISTRESS' *back-of-the-head*)
You notice I *did* say gravesite, and I am not speaking
of an urn of ashes.

THE MISTRESS
(*Small smile*)

I know; I heard you.

THE WIFE
(*Almost apologetic*)

I *will* do battle with you there, no matter what you tell me, no matter what an envelope may say, I will have my way. Not a question of faith, or a repugnance; merely an act of will.

THE MISTRESS
(*Gently*)

Well, I won't argue it with you now.
(THE SON *emerges, closes the door, leans against it, pressed flat, his head up, his eyes toward the ceiling. He is wracked by sobbing, and there is a crumpled handkerchief in his hand*)

THE SON
(*Barely able to get it out, for the sobs*)

It's all . . . still there . . . all . . . just as it . . . was.
(*Quite suddenly he manages to control himself. This effect is not comic. It is clear an immense effort of will has taken place. His voice is not quite steady, falters once or twice, but he is under control*)

I'm sorry; I'm being quite preposterous; I'm sorry. It's just that . . . it's all still there, just as I remember it, not from when I may have seen it last—when? twenty years?—but as it was when I was a child: the enormous sink; the strop; the paneling; the pier glass; the six showerheads and the mosaic tile; and . . . the

. . . the white milkglass bottles with the silver tops, the witch hazel and cologne, the gilt lettering rubbed nearly off; and . . .

> (*Softer; sadder*)

. . . the ivory brushes, and the comb.

> (*Shakes his head rapidly, clearing it; full control*)

Sorry; I'm sorry.

> (*Pause*)

THE WIFE

> (*Sighs, nods several times*)

It would take *you, wouldn't* it. Choose anything, any of the honors, the idea of a face in your mind, something from when he took you somewhere once, or came halfway round the world when you were burning up and the doctors had no way of knowing what it was, then, in those times, sat by your bed the four days till it began to slacken, *then* slept.

> (*Her anger, her contempt, really rising*)

No! Not any of it! Give us you, and you find a BATH-ROOM . . . *MOVING?*

> (*Pause. Softer, a kind defeat*)

Well . . . I can't expect you to be the son of your father and *be* much: it's too great a *burden;* but to be so little is . . .

> (*Dismisses him with a gesture, paces a little*)

You've neither of you had children, thank God, children that I've *known* of.

> (*Harsh*)

I hope you never marry . . . *either* of you!

> (*Softer, if no gentler*)

Let the line end where it is . . . at its zenith.

THE SON
(*A rasped voice*)
Mother! Be kind!

THE WIFE
(*To* THE MISTRESS; *rather fast, almost sing-song*)
We made them both; remember how I told you that he asked me that? If it were true? And how I laughed, and said, oh, yes? Remember?
(THE MISTRESS *nods, without looking at her*)

THE SON
(*Moves toward the stage-left door, stops by* THE DAUGHTER; *speaks to her*)
I'm going across the hall, to the solarium.
(THE WIFE *turns to notice this exchange*)

THE DAUGHTER
(*Without moving*)
All right.

THE SON
So you'll know where I am.

THE DAUGHTER
All right.

THE SON
In case.

THE DAUGHTER
All right.

THE WIFE
(*As* THE SON *reaches the door to the hallway;
mocking, but without vigor*)
Aren't you up to it?

THE SON
(*Mildly; matter-of-fact*)
Not up to you, mother; never was.
(*He exits*)

THE WIFE
(*At something of a loss*)
Well.
(*Pause*)
Well.
(*Pause*)
Indeed.
(THE DAUGHTER *speaks next; while she does,*
THE WIFE *moves about, listening, looking at*
THE DAUGHTER *occasionally, but generally at
furniture, the floor, whatever*)

THE DAUGHTER
(*Never once removing her arm from across
her eyes*)
Dear God, why can't you leave him alone? Why
couldn't you let him be, this *once*. Everyone's the
target of something, something unexpected and maybe
even stupid. You can shore yourself up beautifully,
guns on every degree of the compass, a perfect sur-
round, but when the sky falls in or the earth gives
way beneath your feet . . . so what? It's all untended,
and what's it guarding? Those movies—remember
them?—way back, India, usually, or in the west, the

forts against the savages: the rescue party finally got there, and there was the bastion, guns pricking out from every window and turret, the white caps of the soldiers, the flags of the regiment blowing, but something was wrong; the Max Steiner music had stopped and the only sound was the blowing of the sand; and then the head of the rescue party would shoot off his pistol as a signal to those inside, and wait; still, just the blowing of the sand, and no Max Steiner music; they'd approach, go in, and there it all was, just as all of us except the rescue party knew it would be—every last soldier dead, propped up into position as some kind of grisly joke by the Tughees, or the Sioux, or whatever it was. Why couldn't you have just left him alone? He's spent his grown life getting set against everything, fobbing it all off, covering his shit as best he can, and so what if the sight of one unexpected, ludicrous thing collapses it all? So *what!* It's proof, isn't it? Isn't it proof he's not as . . . little as you said he was? It is, you know.

(*Slight pause*)

You make me as sick as I make you.

(*Pause.* THE WIFE *looks at* THE DAUGHTER *for a little, opens her mouth as if to speak, doesn't, looks back at* THE DOCTOR, *who seems to be dozing, turns to* THE NURSE)

THE WIFE
(*To* THE NURSE)

You . . .

(*Has to clear her throat*)

. . . you'd better go back, I think; he may have fallen asleep.

99

THE NURSE
(*Swivels in her chair, looks back*)
Doubt it; it's a trick he has, allows patients think he
isn't watching.

THE WIFE
(*Abrupt*)
Don't be ridiculous!

THE NURSE
(*Calm*)
Don't be *rude*.

THE WIFE
(*Sincerely*)
I'm sorry.

THE DOCTOR
(*From where he is, without raising his head*)
If I *am* dozing—which *is* possible, though I don't think
I've slept in over forty years—if I *am,* then I imagine
my intuition would snap me back, if anything needed
doing, wouldn't you think? My famous intuition?

THE WIFE
(*Sings it back to him*)
Sor-ry.
(*To* THE MISTRESS; *wryly*)
That's all I seem to say. Shall I apologize to you for
anything?

THE MISTRESS
(*Smiles; shakes her head*)
No thank you.

THE WIFE

I may—just automatically—so pay no attention.

THE MISTRESS
(*Stretches*)
You *could* answer my question, though.

THE WIFE

Have I forgotten it?

THE MISTRESS

Probably. I was wondering, musing: If I had been *you*—the little girl you were when he came to you— would you have come along as I did? Would *you* have come to take *my* place?

THE WIFE
(*Smiles as she thinks about it*)
Hmmmmm. No; I don't think so. We function so differently. I function as a wife, and you—don't misunderstand me—you do not. Married twice, yes, you were, but I doubt your husbands took a mistress, for you were *that,* too. And no man who has a mistress for his wife will take a wife as mistress.
(THE MISTRESS *laughs, softly, gaily*)
We're different kinds; whether I had children or not, I would always be a wife and mother, a symbol of stability rather than refuge. Both your husbands were married before they met you, no?

THE MISTRESS

Um; yes.

101

THE WIFE
(*Light*)

Perhaps you're evil.

THE MISTRESS

No, I don't think so; I never scheme; I have never sought a man out, said, I think I will have this one. Oh, *is* he married? *I* see; well, no matter, that will fall like a discarded skin. I am not like that at all. I have cared for only three men—my own two husbands . . . and yours. My, how shocking that sounds. Well, three men and one boy. That was back, very far, fifteen and sixteen. God!, we were in love: innocent, virgins, both of us, and I doubt that either of us had ever told a lie. We met by chance at a lawn party on a Sunday afternoon, and had got ourselves in bed by dusk. You may not call that love, but it was. We were not embarrassed children, awkward and puppy-rutting. No; fifteen and sixteen, and never been before, but our sex was a strong and practiced and assisting . . . "known" thing between us, from the very start. Fumbling, tears, guilt? No, not a bit of it. He was the most . . . beautiful person I have ever seen: a face I will not try to describe, a lithe, smooth swimmer's body, and a penis I could not dismiss from my mind when I was not with him—I am not one of your ladies who pretends these things are of no account. We were a man and woman . . . an uncorrupted man and woman, and we made love all the summer, every day, wherever, whenever.

(*Pause*)

And then it stopped. *We* stopped.

THE DAUGHTER
(*After a moment; same pose*)
What happened? Something tragic? Did he die, or become a priest?

THE MISTRESS
(*Ignoring her tone; remembering*)
No, nothing like it. We had to go back to school.

THE DAUGHTER
(*Snorts*)
Christ!

THE MISTRESS
We had to go back to *school*. Could anything be simpler?

THE DAUGHTER
(*Raising herself half-up on her elbows;
mildly unpleasant tone*)
No burning correspondence, love and fidelity sworn to eternity? Surely a weeping farewell, holding hands, staring at the ceiling, swearing your passion until Christmas holidays.

THE MISTRESS
(*Still calm*)
No, not that at all. We made love, our last day together, kissed, rather as a brother and *sister* might, and said: "Goodbye; I love you." "Goodbye; I love you."

THE DAUGHTER
A couple of horny kids, that's all.

THE MISTRESS
(Smiles a little)

No, I think you're wrong there. Oh, we were *that*, certainly, but I also think we were very wise. "Leave it; don't touch it again." I told you; it was very simple: we had to go back to school; we were *children*.

THE DAUGHTER
(Reciting the end of a fairy tale)

And you never saw him again.

THE MISTRESS

True. He was from across the country, had been visiting that summer.

THE WIFE
(Very nice)

What became of him?

THE MISTRESS
(Waves it away)

Oh . . . things, things I've read about from time to time; nothing.

THE DAUGHTER

Oh, come on! What became of him!?

THE MISTRESS
(Irritated, but by the questioner, not the question)

Whatever you like! He died and became a priest! *What* do *you* care?

THE DAUGHTER

I don't.

THE MISTRESS

Then shut it up.
>   (THE DAUGHTER *sinks back to her previous
>   position*)

THE WIFE
>   (*After a pause*)

Four men, then.

THE MISTRESS

Hm? Oh; well, yes; yes, I suppose he *was* a man. Four men, then. Not too bad, I guess; spread out, not all bunched together.

THE WIFE

Yes.
>   (*Slowly; something of a self-revelation*)
I have loved only . . . once.

THE MISTRESS
>   (*Nods, smiles; kindly*)

Yes.

THE BEST FRIEND
>   (*Swings around*)

What if there *is* no paper? What if all the envelopes are business, and don't say a thing about it? What if there *are* no instructions?

THE WIFE
>   (*Dry, but sad*)

Then it is in the hands of the wife . . . is it not?

THE BEST FRIEND
Yes, certainly, but . . . still.

THE WIFE
(*On her guard*)

Still?

THE BEST FRIEND
(*Pained*)
After a time, it . . . after a time the prerogative becomes *only* legal.

THE WIFE
Only, and *legal?* Those two words *next* to each other? From you?

THE BEST FRIEND
(*Helpless*)
I can't stop you.

THE WIFE
Why would you want to, and why are we playing "what if"? He's a thorough man, knows as much law as you, or certainly *some* things. I am not a speculator.

THE BEST FRIEND
Those envelopes are not from yesterday.

THE WIFE
I dare say not. How *old* were you when you became aware of death?

THE BEST FRIEND
Well . . . what it meant, you mean.

(*Smiles, remembering*)
The age we all become philosophers—fifteen?

THE WIFE
(*Mildly impatient; mildly amused*)
No, no, when you were aware of it for yourself, when you knew you were at the top of the roller-coaster ride, when you knew half of it was probably over and you were on your *way* to it.

THE BEST FRIEND
Oh.
(*Pause*)
Thirty-eight?

THE WIFE
Did you make a will then?

THE BEST FRIEND
(*A rueful smile*)
Yes.

THE WIFE
Instructions in it?

THE BEST FRIEND
(*Curiously angry*)
Yes! But not about that! Not about what was to be *done* with me. Maybe that's something women think about more.

THE WIFE
(*Surprised, and grudging a point*)
May-*be*.

107

THE BEST FRIEND
(*He, too*)

And maybe it's something I never thought to *think* about.

THE WIFE

Do I sound absolutely *tribal?* Am I wearing feathers and mud, and *are* my earlobes halfway to my shoulders? I wonder! My rationale has been perfectly simple: you may lose your husband while he is alive, but when he is not, then he is yours again.

THE DAUGHTER
(*Same position*)

He still *is.*
(THE WIFE *opens her mouth to reply, stops herself*)

THE BEST FRIEND

What.

THE DAUGHTER

Alive.

THE BEST FRIEND
(*Controlling his anger*)

We *know* that.

THE DAUGHTER

Wondered; that's all.

THE MISTRESS
(*Gently*)

Let's not talk about it any more. We're misunderstood.

108

THE BEST FRIEND

It's just that . . . well, never mind.

THE WIFE
(*Nicely*)

That you're his best friend in the world, and you care about what happens to him?

THE BEST FRIEND
(*Glum*)

Something like that.

THE WIFE

Well, there are a number of his best friends here, and we all seem quite concerned. That we differ is incidental.

THE BEST FRIEND

Hardly. I warn you: if there *is* no paper, and I doubt there is, and you persist in having your way, I'll take it to court.

THE WIFE
(*Steady*)

That will take a long time.

THE BEST FRIEND

No doubt.

THE WIFE

Well.
(*Pause*)
It was pleasant having you as my lawyer.

109

THE BEST FRIEND

Don't be like that.

THE WIFE

(*Furious*)

Don't *be* like that!? Don't *be* like that!? We are talking
of *my husband*. Surely you've not forgotten. You were
a guest in our house—in the days when we *had* a
house together. We entertained you. Here! You and
your wife spent Christmas with us; many times! Who
remembered to bring you your cigars from Havana
whenever we were there? Who went shopping with you
to surprise your wife, to help you make sure it was
right and not the folly you husbands make of so many
things? Me! *Wife!* Remember!?

> (THE BEST FRIEND *goes to her where she sits,*
> *kneels beside her, takes her hands, puts them*
> *to his lips*)

I think I shall cry.

THE BEST FRIEND

No, now.

THE WIFE

(*Wrenches her hands free, looks away; weary*)

Do what you want with him; cast him in bronze if
you like. I won't do battle with you: I like you both
too much.

THE MISTRESS

I told you what he wants, that's all, or what he wanted
when he told me. Let's not fall out over the future.

THE BEST FRIEND
(*Gentle*)
If I retract, will you hire me back again?

THE WIFE
You were never fired; what would I do without you?
Rhetoric.

THE DAUGHTER
(*Same position*)
Join hands; kiss; sing.

THE WIFE
(*Rather light tone, to* THE BEST FRIEND)
What *is* it if you kill your daughter? It's matricide if
she kills *you,* and infanticide if you do her when she's
a tot, but what if she's all grown up and begins to
wrinkle? Justifiable homicide, I suppose.
(THE NURSE *half emerges from behind the
screen*)

THE NURSE
Doctor!?
(*He joins her, and they are only partially
visible.* THE WIFE *stays where she is, grips
the arms of her chair, closes her eyes.* THE
MISTRESS *rises, stays put.* THE BEST FRIEND
moves toward the bed. THE DAUGHTER *rises,
stays where she is*)

THE NURSE
(*Reappearing*)
Stay back; it's nothing for you.
(*She goes back to the bed.*

111

THE MISTRESS *sits again;* THE BEST FRIEND *goes into a chair.* THE DAUGHTER *returns to her sofa*)

THE DAUGHTER
(*She pounds her hands on the sofa, more or less in time to her words; her voice is thick, and strained and angry. She must speak with her teeth clenched*)
Our Father, who art in heaven; hallowed be thy name; thy kingdom come, thy will be done on earth as it is in heaven; give us this day!
(*They are all silent.*
THE NURSE *reappears; her uniform is spotted with blood, as if someone had thrown some at her with a paint brush. There is blood on her hands, too*)

THE NURSE
It's all right; it's a hemorrhage, but it's all right.

THE WIFE
(*Eyes still closed*)
Are you certain!

THE NURSE
(*Forceful, to quiet them*)
It's all right!
(*She returns to the bed*)

THE MISTRESS
(*To* THE WIFE, *after a pause*)
Tell me about something; talk to me about anything—anything!

THE WIFE
(*Struggling for a subject*)
We . . . uh . . . the . . . the garden, yes, the garden
we had, when we had our house in the country, outside
of Paris. We were in France for nearly three years.
Did you . . . did he tell you that?

THE MISTRESS
Yes; was it lovely?

THE WIFE
He couldn't, he couldn't have taken you there. It was
lovely; it burned down; they wrote us.

THE MISTRESS
What a pity.

THE WIFE
Yes; it was lovely.
(*She struggles to get through it*)
It wasn't just a garden; it was a world . . . of . . .
floration. Is that a word? No matter. It was a world
of what it was. One didn't walk out into a garden—in
the sense of when they say to you: "Come see what
we've done." None of any of that. Of *course*. It had
been planned, by careful minds—a woman *and* a man,
I think, for it was that kind, or several; generations—
and it resembled nothing so much as an environment.
(*Head back, loud, to* THE DOCTOR *and* THE
NURSE)
IS ANYONE TELLING ME THE TRUTH!?

THE NURSE
(*Reappearing briefly*)

Yes.

(*Goes back*)

THE WIFE
(*Quietly*)

Thank you.

THE MISTRESS

The garden.

THE WIFE

Yes.

(*Pause, while she regathers*)

The . . . the house, itself, was centuries old, rather Norman on the outside, wood laid into plaster, but not boxy in the Norman manner, small, but rambling; stone floors; huge, simple mantels, great timbers in the ceilings, a kitchen the size of a drawing room—*you* know. And all about it, clinging to it, spreading in every way, a tamed wilderness of garden. No, not tamed; planned, a planned wilderness. Such profusion, and all the birds and butterflies from miles around were privy to it. *And* the bees. One could walk out and make bouquets Redon would have envied.

(*Pause*)

I don't think I want to talk about it any more.

(THE DOCTOR *appears, finishing drying his hands with a towel. He comes forward*)

THE DOCTOR

Close, but all right; there's no predicting those. May I join you?

(*He sits with* THE WIFE *and* THE MISTRESS)
That's better. I suddenly feel quite old . . .
        (*Chuckles*)
. . . which could pass for a laugh, couldn't it?

THE MISTRESS
Are you going to retire, one day?

THE DOCTOR
Couldn't, now; I'm way past retirement age. I should
have done it fifteen years ago. Besides, what would
I do?

THE WIFE
        (*Not looking at* THE DOCTOR)
Did it . . . hasten it?

THE DOCTOR
        (*Pause*)
Sure. What else would you expect? Every breath dimin-
ishes; each heartbeat is taking a chance.

THE MISTRESS
        (*An attempt to change the subject*)
I've never understood how you doctors stay so well in
the midst of it all—the contagions. You must rattle
from the pills and be a mass of pricks.

THE DOCTOR
Oh, it's easier now; used to be a day, though. Still, it's
interesting. In Europe, in the time of the black plague
—and I *read* about it, don't be thinking fresh—when
eighty percent of a town would go, wiped out in a
week, the doctors, such as they were, would lose only

115

half. There wasn't much a doctor could do, in those days, against the bubonic—and especially the pneumonic—but saddling up and running wouldn't have helped, postponed, maybe, so they stayed, tried to get the buboes to break, nailed some houses shut with all the living inside if there was a case, and preceded the priests by a day or two in their rounds. The priests had the same break as the doctors, the same percentages. Might *mean* something; probably not.
> (*Pause*)

Want some more history?

THE WIFE
> (*Shakes her head, smiles a little*)

No.

THE MISTRESS
> (*Ibid.*)

Not really.

THE DOCTOR
> (*Rises, with an effort*)

I'll go back, then. If you do, let me know; I'm up on it.
> (*Starts back, passes* THE DAUGHTER, *recumbent*)

Got a headache, or something?
> (*Moves on*)

THE DAUGHTER
> (*Rises, swiftly; under her breath*)

Christ!
> (*Generally*)

I'll be in the solarium, too.

(She exits, slamming the door after her.
Some silence)

THE WIFE
(To THE MISTRESS, *gently)*
What *will* you do?

THE MISTRESS
(Smiles sadly)
I don't *know*. I've *thought* about it, of course, and
nothing seems much good. I'm not a drinker, and
I'm far too old for drugs. I've thought of taking a
very long trip, of going places I've not been before—
we've not been—but there's quite a lot against that,
too. Do I want to forget, or do I want to remember?
If the choice comes down to masochism or cowardice,
then maybe best do nothing. Though, I must do *some-*
thing. The sad thing is, I've seen so many of them,
the ones who are suddenly without their men, going
back to places they have known together, sitting on
terraces and looking about. They give the impression
of wanting to be recognized, as if the crowd in Cannes
that year had all the people from the time before and
someone would come and say hello. They overdress,
which is something they never would have done before: at three in the afternoon they're wearing frocks,
and evening jewelry, and their make-up is for the dim
of the cocktail lounge, and not the sun. I'm not talking
of the women who fall apart. No, I mean the straight
ladies who are mildly startled by everything, as if something they could not quite place were not quite right.
Well, it is all the things they have come there to not
admit—that the present is not the past, that they must
order for themselves, and trust no one. And the groups

are even worse, those three or four who make the
trips together, those coveys of bewildered widows, talking about their husbands as if they'd gone to a stag,
or were at the club. There's a coarsening in that, a
lack of respect for oneself, ultimately. I *shall* go away;
I *know* that; but it won't be to places unfamiliar,
either. There are different kinds of pain, and being
once more where one has been, and shared, *must* be
easier than being where one *cannot* ever . . . I think
what I shall do is go to where I've been, *we've* been,
but I shall do it out of focus, for indeed it will be.
I'll go to Deauville in October, with only the Nor-
mandie open, and take long, wrapped-up walks along
the beach in the cold and gray. I'll spend a week in
Copenhagen when the Tivoli's closed. And I'll have my
Christmas in Venice, where I'm told it usually snows.
Or maybe I'll just go to Berlin and stare at the wall.
We were there when they put it up. There's so much
one can do. And so little.

   (*Long pause; finally, with tristesse*)
What will *you* do?

      THE WIFE
      (*Pause*)
It's very different. I've been practicing widowhood for
so many years that I don't know what effect the fact
will have on me. Maybe none. I've settled in to a life
which is comfortable, interesting, and useful, and I
contemplate no change. You never know, though. It
may be I have told myself . . . all lies and I am no
more prepared for what will happen—when? tonight?
tomorrow morning?—than I would be were he to
shake off the coma, rise up from his bed, put his arms
about me, ask my forgiveness for all the years, and

take me back. I can't predict. I know I want to feel something. I'm waiting to, and I have no idea what I'm storing up. You make a lot of adjustments over the years, if only to avoid being eaten away. Anger, resentment, loss, self-pity—*and* self-loathing—loneliness. You can't live with all that in the consciousness very long, so, you put it under, *or* it gets well, and you're never sure which. Worst might be if there's nothing there any more, if everything has been accepted. I'm not a stoic by nature, by any means—I would have killed for my children, back when I cared for them, and he could please me and hurt me in ways so subtle and complex I was always more amazed at *how* it had happened than I was by *what*. I remember once: we were in London, for a conference, and, naturally, he was very busy.
(Pause)
No; I don't want to talk about *that,* either. Something *must* be stirring: it's the second time I've balked.

THE MISTRESS
(Nicely)

You won't mind.

THE WIFE
Well, I won't know till it's too late, will I?
(Turns to THE BEST FRIEND)
You're going to ask me to marry you, *aren't* you.

THE BEST FRIEND
(From where he sits)
Certainly.

119

THE WIFE
(*Smiles*)
And I shall *refuse,* shall I *not.*

THE BEST FRIEND
Certainly; I'm no bargain.

THE WIFE
Besides; fifty years married to one man, I wouldn't be
settling on three or four with another—or even ten, if
you outwit all the actuaries. And besides—though
listen to how it sounds from someone *my* age, *my*
condition—I am devoted to you, sir, but I am not in
love with you. Fill my mouth with mould for having
said it, but I love my husband.

THE MISTRESS
(*Smiles, nicely*)
Of course you do.

THE BEST FRIEND
(*As if nothing else had entered his mind and
he is not disputing it*)
Of course you do.

THE WIFE
(*A bit put off by their acquiescence*)
Yes. Well.
(*Shakes her head, slowly, sadly*)
Oh, God; the little girl.
(*Does she move about? Perhaps*)
Eighteen . . .
(*To* THE MISTRESS)

and none of yours, no summer lovemaking; no thought
to it, or anything like it; alas.
(*Pause, gathers herself again*)
Some would-be beaux, but, like myself, tongue-tied
and very much their ages. They would come to call,
drink lemonade with my mother there, an aunt or so,
an uncle; they would take me walking, play croquet,
to a dance. I didn't fancy any of them.

THE MISTRESS
(*Smiles*)
No; you were waiting.

THE WIFE
(*Shakes her head, laughs*)
Of course! For Prince Charming!
(THE MISTRESS *chuckles.* THE WIFE *shrugs*)
And then—of course—he came *along,* done with the
university, missing the war in France, twenty-four,
already started on his fortune—just begun, but straight
ahead, and clear. We went at my rich uncle's house,
where he had come to discuss a proposition, and he
made me feel twelve again, or younger, and . . . comfortable, as if he were an older brother, though . . .
different; very different. I had never felt threatened, by
boys, but he was a man, and I felt secure.

THE MISTRESS
Did you fall in love at once?

THE WIFE
Hm?
(*Thinks about it*)
I don't *know;* I knew that I would marry him, that he

121

would ask me, and it seemed very . . . right. I felt calm.
Is that an emotion? I suppose it is.

THE MISTRESS

Very much.

THE WIFE
(Sighs heavily)
And two years after that we were married; and thirty
years later . . . he met *you*. Quick history. Ah, well.
(A quickening)
Perhaps if I had been . . .
(Realizes)
No; I don't suppose so.
(A silence)

THE DOCTOR
(Emerging from where the bed has hidden
him; to THE BEST FRIEND)
Where are the others?

THE BEST FRIEND
(Rising)
In the solarium.

THE DOCTOR
(Level)
You'd best have them come in.

THE WIFE
(Pathetic; lost)
No-o!

THE BEST FRIEND
(*Moving toward the door; to* THE DOCTOR)
I'll get them.

THE WIFE
(*Ibid.*)
Not yet!

THE BEST FRIEND
(*Misunderstanding*)
They should *be* here.

THE WIFE
(*Ibid.*)
I don't mean them!

THE BEST FRIEND
(*Hard to breathe*)
I'll get them.

(*He exits*)

THE WIFE
(*Turning back to* THE DOCTOR; *as before;
pathetic, lost*)
Not yet!

THE MISTRESS
(*Takes* THE WIFE's *hand*)
Shhhhhhhhh; be a rock.

THE WIFE
(*Resentful*)
Why!

THE MISTRESS

They need you to.

THE WIFE
(*Almost sneering*)

Not you?

THE MISTRESS
(*Matter-of-fact*)

I'll manage. It would help, though.

THE WIFE
(*Takes her hand away; hard*)

You be; *you* be the rock. I've *been* one, for all the years; steady. It's profitless!

THE MISTRESS

Then, just a little longer.

THE WIFE
(*Almost snarling*)

You be; *you've* usurped!
(*Pause; finally; still hard*)

I'm sorry!

THE MISTRESS

That's not fair.

THE WIFE
(*Still hard*)

Why? Because I no longer had what you up and took?

THE MISTRESS
(*Her tone hard, too*)

Something like that.

124

THE WIFE
(*A sudden, hard admitting, the tone strong, but with loss*)
I don't love *you*.
(THE MISTRESS *nods, looks away*)
I don't love *anyone*.
(*Pause*)
Any more.
(*The door opens;* THE DAUGHTER *enters, followed by* THE SON, *followed by* THE BEST FRIEND. THE BEST FRIEND *moves wearily, the other two shy, as if they were afraid that by making a sound or touching anything the world would shatter.* THE BEST FRIEND *quietly closes the door behind him; the other two move a few paces, stand there.*
On her feet, now; to THE DAUGHTER, *same tone as before*)
I don't love *you*,
(*To* THE SON)
and I don't love *you*.

THE BEST FRIEND
(*Quietly*)
Don't do that.

THE WIFE
(*Quieter, but merciless*)
And you know I don't love *you*.
(*An enraged shout which has her quivering*)
I LOVE MY HUSBAND!!
(THE NURSE *has moved forward;* THE DAUGHTER *moves to her, buries herself in* THE

NURSE's *arms.* THE SON *falls into a chair,
covers his face with his hands, sobs.
To* THE SON)

STOP IT!!

(THE SON *abruptly ceases his sobbing, doesn't
move*)

THE MISTRESS
(*Steady*)

You stop it.

(*Silence;* THE BEST FRIEND *moves to the fireplace;* THE MISTRESS *and* THE WIFE *are both
seated;* THE SON *stays where he is;* THE
DAUGHTER *returns to the sofa;* THE DOCTOR
is by the bed; THE NURSE *stands behind the
sofa and to one side, eyes steady, ready to
assist or prevent. Nobody moves from these
positions, save* THE DOCTOR, *from now until
the end of the play*)

THE WIFE
(*Calm, now, almost toneless. A slow speech,
broken with long pauses*)

All we've done . . . is think about ourselves.

(*Pause*)

There's no help for the dying. I suppose. Oh my;
the burden.

(*Pause*)

What will become of *me* . . . and *me* . . . and *mē*.

(*Pause*)

Well, we're the ones have got to go on.

(*Pause*)

Selfless love? *I* don't think so; we love to *be* loved, and

126

when it's taken away . . . then why *not* rage . . . or
pule.

(*Pause*)

All we've *done* is think about ourselves. Ultimately.
(*A long silence. Then* THE WIFE *begins to
cry. She does not move, her head high, eyes
forward, hands gripping the arms of her
chair. First it is only tears, but then the
sounds in the throat begin. It is controlled
weeping, but barely controlled*)

THE DAUGHTER

(*After a bit; not loud, but bitter and ac-
cusatory*)

Why are you crying!

THE WIFE

(*It explodes from her, finally, all that has
been pent up for thirty years. It is loud,
broken by sobs and gulps of air; it is self-
pitying and self-loathing; pain, and relief*)

Because . . . I'm . . . unhappy.

(*Pause*)

Because . . . I'm . . . unhappy.

(*Pause*)

BECAUSE . . . I'M . . . UNHAPPY!

(*A silence, as she regains control. Then she
says it once more, almost conversational, but
empty, flat*)

Because I'm unhappy.

(*A long silence. No one moves, save* THE
DOCTOR, *who finally removes the stethoscope
from* THE PATIENT's *chest, then from his*

ears. He stands, pauses for a moment, then walks a few steps forward, stops)

THE DOCTOR
(Gently)

All over.

(No one moves)

END